B. W. Flint

Rose of Normandie

Published by

LANTERN TOWER

An Imprint of Melrose Press Limited
St Thomas Place, Ely
Cambridgeshire
CB7 4GG, UK
www.melrosebooks.com

FIRST EDITION

ISBN 978 1 907040 02 3

Printed and bound in Great Britain by:
CPI Antony Rowe, Chippenham, Wiltshire

FSC
Mixed Sources
Product group from well-managed
forests and other controlled sources
Cert no. SGS-COC-2953
www.fsc.org
© 1996 Forest Stewardship Council

Foreword

THERESE OF LISIEUX IS A SAINT WHO speaks powerfully to our present age. A young woman, who in her short life, grasped that God was calling her to be love in the heart of the Church. Her insights came through her ability to trust wholeheartedly in God, despite illness and at times temptations to doubt the very essence of her calling. Interest in St Therese will be heightened as her relics come to England and it is in this context that Bill Flint's book *The Rose of Normandie* will be welcomed. Therese is best known for her autobiography *Story of a Soul* which gives amazing insights into her inner life. *The Rose of Normandie* gives access to her other writings which are only gradually becoming known in English. Bill Flint introduces us to these writings along with his own reactions. The result of this process is a series of creative meditations which reveal the richness and scope of the Saint's writings and the effect they have had on Bill Flint. Perhaps this presentation will challenge us to know Therese more fully and see the richness of her life and writings. Therese is now a doctor of the Church, a reminder that her writings hold deep significance for those

THE ROSE OF NORMANDIE

who are searching for meaning and a way out of a one-dimensional world.

Father Wilfred McGreal
The English Provincial in charge of the Carmelite order
of Great Britain

iv

JOHN PAUL II PROCLAIMS
SAINT THERESE
DOCTOR OF THE CHURCH

IT WAS ABOUT THIS TIME [1885], THAT the young Sister Therese of the Child Jesus and the Holy Face (her name in religion which sums up her vocation) discovered the way of spiritual childhood after years of searching. It was to change her life. She received the grace of a deeper understanding of God's paternity which is nothing but Merciful Love (expressed in His incarnate Son, Jesus). Christian life is nothing other than living as a child of the Father ("as sons in the son") starting at Baptism and continued in absolute trust. "If you do not become like little children, you will not enter the Kingdom of Heaven," says Jesus **(Matthew 18:3).**

She had written that she wanted to be "a priest, a deacon, a prophet, a doctor (of the Church), a missionary, a martyr…" in a word, everything. She had discovered her vocation was to be "Love in the heart of the Church," her mother.

"I came (to Carmel) to save souls and especially to pray for priests. **(Ms A, 69 vo)**

"Considering the mystical body of the Church, I had not recognized myself in any of the members described by Saint Paul; or rather I desired to see myself in them all. Charity gave me the key to my vocation. I understood that if the Church had a body composed of different members, the most necessary and the most noble of all could not be lacking to it, and so I understood that the Church had a heart and that this heart was BURNING WITH LOVE. I understood that it was Love alone that made the Church's members act, that if love ever became extinct, apostles would not preach the Gospel and martyrs would not shed their blood. I understood that LOVE COMPRISED ALL VOCATIONS, THAT LOVE WAS EVERYTHING, THAT IT EMBRACED ALL TIMES AND PLACES…IN A WORD, THAT IT WAS ETERNAL! Then in the excess of my delirious joy, I cried out: 'O Jesus my Love… my vocation, at last I have found it… MY VOCATION IS LOVE! Yes I have found my place in the Church and it is You) my God, who have given me this place. In the heart of the Church, my mother, I shall be Love. Thus I shall be everything and my dream will be realised.'" **(Ms B 3vo)**

In 1970 a decisive event took place: Pope Paul the VI declared two women, Doctors of the Church: Teresa of Villa and Catherine of Sienna. It was a considerable event and unfortunately we still haven't drawn the conclusions it implied, twenty-seven years on. At the time some asked "What about Therese?"

Saint Thomas of Aquinas shows that there are two ways of speaking of God: the speculative way, which he used and also the metaphorical way. For historical reasons women have mostly used the latter. Two centuries later Teresa of Avila also said she knew nothing. She was even threatened by the

Inquisition. She was saved from this threat and defended by Dominicans and Jesuits who demonstrated that she wasn't mad but that she had a profound contribution to make. For centuries there was much strong anti feminism prejudice prevalent in matters of learning. Women were considered 'ignorant', they had no voice. Saint Joan of Arc suffered the consequences…

However speculation is not the only way of speaking about God and of contributing to insights and profound intuitions to Theology, as Balthasar said. He insists especially on the fact women have gone further in the understanding of and discovery of the concept of Mercy, which lies in the heart of God's mystery.

Therese found the meaning of the Trinity, the meaning of the Incarnation, the bond uniting the Father and the Son. She rediscovered the Church, a place of communion and love where the Holy Spirit comes first. She opened up a new way of sanctity for all, even the poor as long as they trust in God. Because Hope is a fundamental virtue for our world. She returned to a Mariology announcing that of the second Vatican Council, to a Virgin who had faith and who followed her Son from the Annunciation to Calvary.

Despite her lack of training, the lack of resources for studying and interpreting the sacred books, Therese immersed herself in meditation of the Word of God with exceptional faith, intellect and spontaneity. Under the direction and influence of the Holy Spirit she obtained a profound knowledge of Revelation for herself and for all she teaches. By her loving concentration on Scripture, she desired to learn Hebrew and Greek to understand better the spirit and the letter of the sacred books. She demonstrates the importance of the Biblical sources in the spiritual life. She emphasized the originality and freshness of the Gospel. She cultivated with great skill the spiritual exegesis of the Word of God in both the Old and New Testaments. Thus she discovered hidden treasures, appropriating words and episodes sometimes with great boldness and understanding. As when in reading the texts of St Paul **(cf 1 Corinthians 12 – 13)** she realized her vocation to Love **(cf Ms B3 ro-3vo)**. Enlightened by the revealed Word, Therese wrote brilliant pages on the unity between the Love of God and the Love of neighbour **(cf Ms C, 11vo-19rc)**; and she identified with Jesus' prayer at the Last Supper as the expression of her intercession for the salvation of all. **(Ms C, 34ro-35vo)**

Therese is not only the youngest Doctor of the Church but is also the closest to us in time as if to emphasize the continuity with which the Spirit of The Lord sends his messengers to the church, both women and men as teachers and witnesses to the Faith. In fact whatever changes can be noted in the course of History and despite their varied repercussions that they usually have on the life and thought of individuals in every age, we must never lose sight of the continuity which links the Doctors of the Church to each other. In every historical context they remain witnesses to the unchanging Gospel and with the life and strength which comes from the Holy Spirit they become its messengers, returning to proclaim in its purity to their contemporaries. Therese is a teacher for our time, which thirsts for living and essential words, for heroic and credible acts of witness. For this reason she is loved and accepted by brothers and sisters of other Christian communities and even by non Christians. (…)

B. W. Flint

*"TODAY, THE 19TH OF OCTOBER
1997, IN ST PETER'S SQUARE,
FILLED WITH FAITHFUL
FROM EVERY PART OF THE
WORLD, IN THE PRESENCE OF
A GREAT MANY CARDINALS,
ARCHBISHOPS AND BISHOPS
DURNG THE SOLEMN
EUCHARISTIC CELEBRATION
I PROCLAIMED THERESE OF
THE CHILD JESUS AND THE
HOLY FACE A DOCTOR OF THE
CHURCH."*

John Paul II.

ix

Our Lord has given me insight and reached down to me to explain this enigmatic mystery. So I came to know that every flower created by him is sublimely beautiful. That the brilliant colour of the rose and the alabaster whiteness of the lily does not detract from the perfumed intensity of the humble violet. The sweet intense simplicity of the daisy or the drab rust of the ragwort dandelion. It became clear to me in my understanding that all the seasons have their beautiful garments. The panel enamel hills and fields would lose their beautiful embroidered appearance like silk embroidered thread fabrics, a coat of many colours, if the smallest and most drab were removed from their colour palette.

It is the same in this world of souls, for we are Our Lord's living garment. He has nurtured great saints likened unto the lily and the rose yet he lovingly cares for the most humble and simple and all the mortality of death decay and renewal. For all creation is his doing and in their varied incompleteness, the meadows and the fields, the woods and all humankind do his will. Though they flourish fitfully the greater is their perfection however hesitant and brief. I have understood that God's love is made manifest to the poor and simple who do not resist his grace; just as much as to those who are richly endowed. In fact as the most beautiful characteristic is self-effacement then the most hidden and lowliest of creatures are a special delight to him who knows all creatures most intimately. He has made the little child who knows nothing and can only gurgle, and many ignorant who have only the natural law to guide them. It is to them in their hearts that he stoops whose simplicity delights him. They have his eternal love!

INTRODUCTION

THE LIFE STORY OF THERESE THE YOUNGEST child of Louis Martin and his wife Zelie Guerin spans only twenty-five years at the close of the nineteenth century. It was a time of great change and the modern world of trains and wonderful inventions like the escalator were changing forever the urban city life and creating great wealth in foreign trade, manufacturing and transport by land and sea. These advances made possible by science and applied engineering inspired the imagination of Therese even as an enclosed Carmelite nun.

Her story is that of an international star whose teaching and life lived in seclusion and much prayer has illuminated the world for a century. She was born the ninth child of most loving and devout parents at 42 Rue St Blaise, in the town of Alencon in southern Normandy. Her brothers all died in infancy and the remaining family of five sisters were a very close and loving coterie. They were brought even closer when their mother died in 1877, when Therese was only four years old. This made the loving bond of affection between Therese and her father very close.

Her parents had been married for nearly twenty-four

years and Zelie was nearing her forties when her youngest child was born. Her eldest sisters in their late teens were at home on their Christmas holidays from the Convent of the Visitation in Le Mans when she was born on January 2nd 1873. Her eldest sister Marie became her Godmother. Her sister Pauline who entered the Carmel in Lisieux some years before Therese became her Mother Superior in later years. It was on the instructions of Pauline as her Mother Superior that she wrote her wonderful autobiographical works which are the carpet meadow foundations for this work.

The first part of the manuscript (Part One) is dedicated to her sister Pauline as Mother Superior in the name of her religious persona '*Mother Agnes of Jesus*'. The second manuscript (Part Two) is dedicated to '*Mother Marie Gonzaga*' who succeeded Pauline as Mother Superior. The third and last manuscript is dedicated to Marie her eldest sister and Godmother, addressed as '*Marie of the Sacred Heart*'. It is a most intimate appreciation of the 'Heart of Love', inspired by her lifelong devotion to understanding and emulating the young girls of the 'Song of Songs' it is entitled *A Canticle of Love*!

The manuscripts were not written in chapters or a book format. Some of the passages are written in a very fine French prose style and we are delighted at the vivid and learned metaphysics of much of her wonderful poetry. Her writings have never been revised although written with great rapidity; she is clearly a woman of great intellect and is a wonderful adornment of the pantheon of great French writers and poets. Her writings reveal a biblical scholar of great worth and her Title of '*Doctor of the Church*' is a tribute to her great learning and knowledge of the sacred books.

The first and longest of the manuscripts was given the title by her of *'The Little White Flower'*. Thus we are drawn to her description of the daisies of the meadows, open faced smiling up to the heavens yet adorning the fields of this earth.

After the early death of his wife Louis Martin moved his family from Alencon to Lisieux in upper Normandie. The town has an ancient association with William the Conqueror and has ancient family links to many of the English aristocracy. It is in a most tranquil and beautiful region in the valley of the Toques amidst ancient apple orchards and verdant pastures. They arrived in the town in 1877 where the Guerin family lived. The two branches of the marriage families were very close. As a widower in poor health Therese's father relied much upon the counsel and closeness of his in-laws. Sister Therese entered into the Carmel in Lisieux at the age of fifteen under a special dispensation from the local Bishop.

She died there on September 30th 1897 in her twenty-fifth year. She was totally unknown to the wide world yet much loved and cherished by all who knew her. They treasured her life among them as a true sign of God's love for all. Especially the little ones who like the daisy are often overlooked and trampled underfoot.

William Conner Flint.

ACKNOWLEDGEMENTS

To the unenclosed novices of Filton, whom Saint Therese
teaches and charms;
Father Patrick O'Donovan, our promoter in faith;
Linda Hogan, whose tireless work merits much in heaven;
Tessa, Bridie, Alice, Richard et al.

All these faithful are a family Blessed by the Virgin Mother,
taught by Saint Therese and watched over, His little flock, by
Jesus, Shepherd of all Creation.
There in the Crypt, we have sung His praises.

Saint Therese of the Child Jesus, Her church in Filton

A Morning Offering

O MY GOD, I OFFER TO YOU ALL my actions during this day for the Glory of the Sacred Heart of Jesus.

I desire to sanctify every beat of my heart, every thought, my simplest works, by uniting them to its infinite merits and I want to make reparation for my sins by casting them into the furnace of its merciful love!

O my God, I ask you for myself and for all those whom I hold dear, the grace to fulfil, perfectly, your Holy Will and to accept for the Love of Thee, the joys and sorrows of this passing life so that one day we may be united altogether in heaven for all eternity.

Amen.

NB: The original manuscript is preserved at the national shrine of Scotland at Carfin.

FOREWORD

THIS LITTLE WORK INTRODUCES THE LIFE AND teachings of Saint Therese of Lisieux and was inspired by the workings of the Holy Spirit through the prayers of the Parish of Saint Therese of the Child Jesus at Filton in Bristol. Much is owed to the leadership, inspiration and encouragement of our Parish Priest, Father Patrick O'Donovan.

Our scriptural study group began in September 1989 and some years later the Parish Prayer of Saint Therese was inspired as part of the 'Little Way' of love.

It was not until July 1999, following a Parish Pilgrimage to Lisieux, that I was called to Join the scriptural study group, a study of the Saint's teachings now that she was a 'Doctor of the Church'.

Through Deborah's devotion to Our Blessed Lady, together with my daughter's prayers, we visited the Scottish national shrine at Carfin. This shrine is associated closely with the Saint and Doctor of the Church through its founder, the Reverend Thomas N. Taylor. At this shrine there is also the wonderful manuscript with the title 'A Morning Offering'.

Soon after this, on my part reluctant, visit to Saint

Therese at Carfin, I came across the book written by Canon Taylor, *The Little White Flower*, in a second-hand bookshop in Saint Nicholas Market in Bristol. This book, based on the authenticated manuscripts of the Carmelite order, became the basis for our studies and has a special place at the heart of our little community.

I have retranslated parts of the text and also the poem of Saint John of the Cross. It was decided that we would not begin with the Saint's autobiographical writings of her childhood, but rather seek to come to know 'Little Therese' through the anecdotal reminiscences and writings of her sisters in Carmel. The autobiographical manuscripts have been translated and published all round the world. They are a great source of prayer and teaching but essentially different in accent and tone as well as content which is present in the manuscripts written to Mother Gonzaga as assistant 'Novice Mistress', Missionary with the Priesthood and her little doctrine.

We chose to study these works of the Saint in the wonderful knowledge that she is Doctor of the Church; her teachings are most modern, radical and Holy with a theology centred on God's relationship to us as Lover of His Creation. Caught up in this embrace of His love, exemplified in the Song of Songs, Saint Therese teaches us as 'the Beloved'. For we are Beloved of God in the most intimate way through Jesus, the Word made flesh, and the Holy Spirit residing in our hearts.

Saint Therese was unable to identify with the Pauline description of human genius, which forms His mystical Body, the Church. It came to her that her way, the little way, was in being, 'the Heart of the Church'. This heartbeat, ecstatic, quiet, rhythmic and hidden, is yet absolutely essential to the Church's existence. As she wrote, "Without the pulsing heartbeat of love, martyrs would lose courage, Apostles fail to hear the call and the faithful lose heart."

The Doctrine of the 'Little Way', which is now the teaching of the Church, is the bedrock, the foundation of the 'collaborative ministry'. It calls everyone but especially the laity to the profound understanding of being Beloved. In this Belovedness, Saint Therese urges us to look lovingly upon Our Lord and seek to comfort and console Him in His agony of neglect and rejection. He suffered and died in the Crucifixion for all and comes to us always and everywhere, whenever there is a cry from the heart for comfort and consolation. We, Baptised into Him, must come to comfort and console Him for He is true man and true God and longs, indeed thirsts, for the love of those whom He seeks to save. Rather than merely intercede, we should love in place of all those lost and bewildered in the desert of their absorption in this world. In this we will collaborate with all the organs of His mystical body and witness to His loving presence here in the world with us. The little way is the heart of His Church. It is the Sacred Heart alight with love in this world, the world of His incarnation. In every Parish where the seven candles burn with Christ in their midst, the little way should be fostered among His 'little ones', for they are close to Him and He holds them in His heart.

In the last chapter of this little work we outline this collaborative ministry as the work of the Saint and Doctor of His Church.

The Saint teaches also, in a most inspiring way, of her understanding of suffering and self-giving. Love, she teaches, must be totally free of all self-interest; only in this understanding can we, as human beings, reach out in a loving embrace and console the consolation of all mankind, Jesus.

The love of Little Therese was undaunted. No barrier could hold her back from coming to Jesus. She taught us novices to fling our arms about His neck and kiss Him full on the lips, in the knowledge that He returns our kisses full on both cheeks. She went to heaven empty-handed, imploring Jesus to take His love for her, His Beloved, as the only true merit of her existence. Saint Therese taught this novice that the gift of faith is priceless. Only in this life can we love by Faith alone. This is not deprivation but rather the gift of the horn of plenty; for even when we turn away and absorb ourselves in this world, faith folds His arms around us so that we know the heat of love. Faith holds at bay the black night of despair; it lights up our lives and the glories of creation stand in our sight revealed. To live and love by faith is to love truly with such a love as Saint Therese, a love not dependent upon that which delights our eyes, formed in our transient senses. Rather 'true love' which knows that it is 'Beloved' in its very existence, its own self-existence amidst the existence of Our Lover's glory in the existence of all, His Creation! We abandon ourselves to Jesus, for otherwise we abandon ourselves to self-absorption, the chilling emptiness of nothingness. Faith grows firm in our hearts and through the Holy Spirit leads us back through the only Son to the Father.

Faith is the scabbard of the two-edged sword. It is the receptacle of His loving presence calling us home in our hearts. Faith is the remedy for despair, for faith knows first that we are beloved of God and that as Beloved, we are filled with the divine life of the Holy Spirit which unites our own spirit of life to Jesus as Paraclete. This unity of spirit illuminates our minds and sets fire to our hearts and all the darkness of despair is eclipsed with the light of our love, embraced in the virtues of faith and hope.

Faith is a natural response to the human condition because as humans, we love even when Our Lover is not present to our senses. When we cannot see or hear, or touch or taste or smell Our Lover, we continue to love. Beyond the grave in death, we remain 'in love' and continue to act through love with sign and hope in the knowledge that our love is eternal.

Thus all love grows and flourishes out of faith, for it is lovers who murmur 'you will always love me, won't you?' As Beloved, the object of love and the Lover, we thrill with love and know it truly as an act of faith. Broken hearts are the result of love betrayed and it is the human betrayal of God, the Creator's love for us His creatures, which broke the bond of trust and set free the despair of death to rampage in the human heart. Faith, then, is the shield of His love remaining in our existence and understanding even though we fled the garden of Paradise where we walked and talked with God, where we lived as lovers in His presence. As novices we give thanks to our 'Mistress', Little Therese, for her teaching on Faith.

In the Church, Paradise is restored in Jesus' mystical Body because what has been restored to us is the ability to walk and talk with Jesus as lovers in God's presence, the Blessed Sacrament, present in our senses, the Incarnate God, Father, Son and Holy Spirit; or as Saint Therese would always say and write, 'The Spirit of God'.

> *God immanent, Spirit of Love, Fill our hearts with the Song of the Beloved. All her life she sought her Lover. Little Therese, the 'spinning top' of life in colour. The rainbow is the Kaleidoscope of His embrace, Her gift*

to us of her wisdom in the Holy Spirit, the practical
demonstration of Love without dimensions.

For Saint Therese taught this novice that love has no confinement of duration, space or dependence upon contingent relativity, for Love expresses only perfection. The command of Jesus to Love as He loves leads to His other great command, which goes unheralded, 'Be perfect as I am perfect'. We, in the 'little way of love' can only aspire to perfection, as He is perfect, in His perfection. Hence we know His Church as His mystical Body, through which, in which, in Him, as children of God we can come to perfection, in His perfection. His Church is Universal, embracing all and through Baptism, embracing in His perfection the Baptism of desire where the waters flow – the waters of eternal life – sufficient grace for all, perfection awaits us, the essence of His call.

Perfection is the smallest of the little ones and the greatest of which there is no greater. Chaos, nothingness, yes, death can be made perfect in Him for He died for all and He conquered death; that is, He transformed it, having tasted its bitter dregs, by subduing its savage chaotic disintegration, its separation from the goodness of God; He consumed death in the fire of His love and rose in the perfection of the Incarnate God when His disciples beheld the awful wounds of that pinioned struggle. For evil knows nothing. It is powerless to come to love or even know love. So He drew it into Himself, the fire of His transforming love, separated in death from His Father and the Holy Spirit as God, true man. So that in the resurrection, we all are united through Jesus, true God and true man to the Father and the Holy Spirit of love. For us, in Jesus the Christ, God of all Goodness, took on the terrible reality of death that we should have eternal life. We are humble before such suffering in the knowledge that it is the price of the gift of our salvation. We are humble in our littleness. How insignificant are our merits in the vastness of God's love for all Creation.

All sacred power and holiness lead to the Holy Eucharist of the Blessed Sacrament of His Body and Blood. The small white Host, the very presence of His perfection here with us. The cup of His Blood, the Blood of the new and everlasting covenant, poured out for us and all mankind. His Body and Blood, we eat and drink with relish, for with Him in us and us in Him, we tread 'His Way' on the pathway to perfection. Then loving all others as He loves all of us, we keep His commands for love demands that we act! Therese teaches this, her little way, as our way to heaven. However high the mountain and steep the climb, throw yourself into the arms of Christ and know that He will lift you up to Himself in heaven.

As little ones, we cannot mount the stairway of perfection, instead our Little Therese teaches that we offer all in Love, all our failings, all our little triumphs, all our little frustrations, pain and suffering for the sake of others, that they will come and be comforted in Christ. Then without merit, lost in love of Jesus, we hope, on the escalator of His love, for all to be transported up to Him in Heaven.

Saint Therese of Lisieux, Doctor of the Church

Suffering and pain whilst growing in love and goodness toward God, was the staff that accompanied St Therese on her little way of love. Dying so young and suffering so much is remarkable in such a short life. She would never have gone to college and university or started out on a career; her health was too poor. Had she not entered the Convent, it would probably have been said of her that her life was cut short with nothing accomplished and her talents unused. The world and its ways could only view such a truncated life as wasted potential.

On the contrary, the reality of St Therese's life was one of remarkable achievement. She brought peace and joy to many that lived with her and worked with her or just met her. She is a Doctor of the Church, her writings commended to the faithful together with her life as part of the Church's teaching. This reality of a way of life is a lesson in achievement, lasting universal achievement, which witnesses to the truth of the Christian revelation, tradition and teaching.

Saint Therese grew into a spiritual being where her understanding and awareness of existence, through her life as part of a universal vision, gave meaning to pain and suffering. The world we know, 'God's creation', was viewed from a spiritual horizon and the material dimension kept in proper proportion because she caused her pain and suffering to keep materialism at arm's length whilst her spiritual understanding flourished. Her prayer was not a cover or distraction from pain and discomfort, but rather an extension of the awareness of life as a gift from God in loving goodness. As His gift of love, her pain enabled her to concentrate her awareness on God's beautiful gift of creative life. Her suffering was a creative framework to her vision of truth; like a sculptor's chisel creating shape from an indistinguishable lump.

Her bodily presence and affliction was like a growing branch which, sustained and nourished by the love of God in prayer, private and liturgical, put forth leaf and bud and flower in her life – leaf as she tended to and comforted others, bud as her radiance of goodness drew her community to deeper faith and greater fervour in the love of God and flower when she was transformed in prayer and her writing showed forth the wonder and Glory of God in Truth.

She flowers fully in the perfumed miracles that Jesus works through her, for she lived completely in Him as He lived in her. Thus the life of Christ pulsed in her heart, and the pain and suffering were transformed in that process that leads to resurrection – resurrection in Him in a life that flourishes spiritually in the soil of the heart; that is, our lives lived out in holiness, sanctified in Him, His spiritual body, the Church.

How can we come to understand pain and suffering in the light of the life and work of St Therese?

Jesus, in the parable of the Sower, teaches us that He is the Sower and that the seed is His word; that is, His whole life and work, not just the written sentence of the Gospel! The soil is the soil of our hearts; that is, our total life becoming a rich tilth of goodness in which the seed flourishes, or a barrenness of rock, or the hard unyielding surface of a concrete path, or a desert of shallow soil where no root can set down. The rich loam of our hearts can be compared to soil ploughed deep to allow the rain and frost of life's experience to break it up and bring it to the light; then it is harrowed and rolled into a seedbed. The valleys and hills smoothed out for the coming of the Saviour, Jesus the Christ. This seedbed watered by the Sacraments and made warm in the sunlight of His empowering grace is caressed by the breeze of the Holy Spirit. Ready for the Sower then, the seed will flourish and flower.

Pain and suffering, in the light of such a saintly life as St Therese's, focuses our attention on the limitation of the sensual life of the flesh and yet raises our understanding of the dignity of human life as the living ground which is given to us to nourish and maintain our spiritual existence in the perfection of eternal life. This ground is the complex emotional and sensory phenomena, which we call our life.

Ploughing deep and exposing the soil to frost, wind, snow and rain is not an induction process but rather a rigorous training preparation of cleansing and cleaning to ensure that the soil structure and its ability to sustain and promote new growth, and anchor and sustain the root system, is prepared to work effectively. A process of change which enables a stream of nutrients to be released whilst absorbing water and heat then made available again as sources of energy. What appears from superficial observation to be a laceration and pummelling of the soil is in fact a combination of treatments, which make the seedbed fertile.

Human lives are like this when we understand 'the heart' as the seedbed of the living growing person as both a spiritual and physical reality. There is only one unique person in view and only one unique reality. Yet this is the universal understanding of humankind from the time of the Old Testament. In this we can find and know the truth.

Does it follow that pain and suffering are directed toward, or necessary to, conversion? Surely not; for this would attribute to God a prescriptive remedy of hardship that we should come to Him. Conversion of the heart is revealing His law written on our hearts as the creative truth of spiritual life.

It does not follow that all that suffer are brought nearer God, or are hallowed and sanctified as was Saint Therese. For many, suffering is a barrier to loving and serving a loving God. It is rather a shadow on their lives, a limitation and burden to their understanding, for to them it has no purpose. To those poor souls, when pain is known and understood as an integral part of a process of physical or mental healing, then that is understandable and acceptable. This materialistic view avoids all consideration of pain in view of the emotional and spiritual dimension of the human person. When pain is considered in materialistic terms, as pointless and purposeless, then it is offensive to their concept of a loving God. To these poor souls only when pain is known and understood as an integral part of a process of healing, physical or mental, is it understandable and acceptable. This materialistic understanding avoids all consideration of pain as an emotional and physical dimension of the spiritual identity of the human person evolving to the perfection as 'God's creation'. When pain and suffering are considered in the material dimension only then they are offensive to the concept of an all loving God. Defined in the terms of an existence without an eternal dimension God is malevolent, capricious, a God of Olympus. Or they reject all belief in God declaring his non existence or that perhaps God exists only as an infused concept of the good of all things as a basis of temporal morality.

However this belief in an innate goodness is clearly without rational foundation. Knowledge of God cannot be dependent upon human evaluation of His Will and purpose. Even in a process of innate understanding otherwise God becomes an invention of human intelligence and desire!

Pain and suffering are clearly accidents of our complex existence and interaction with others in a material world governed by physical laws which we cannot alter or defy. This physical existence created out of the chaos of nothingness, is drawn to perfection which God gives us; in a separate process of 'necessary grace' the means to enable us and the whole universe to evolve into the perfection of Jesus Christ through the exercise of free will in the fullness of love. We are part of 'God's creation made in His image and likeness, we are the sons and daughters of God and stewards of His work, therefore we have the power through Christ to perfect it in Him and prepare it for his Kingdom.' "All creation groans as if in childbirth" teaches Saint Paul. This demonstrates that the forces of disintegration and decay are at war with the forces of perfection and harmony, the stable states. In this turmoil we can understand the second law of thermodynamics and come to a rational view of pain and suffering as the accidental consequence of this physical and in human nature emotional and spiritual conflict. Life as spirit is known in this in its limited sense spirit confined within the limitations of the known physical law. The Holy Spirit transcends this in human life endowing us with the perfection of eternity. This Living Sprit was traduced by Adam as he tried to grasp the perfection of the Godhead and thereby become God, rather than remain in loving obedience and evolve to the perfection of eternity with God as loving subjects of the Kingdom. This has now been accomplished through Christ through Him and with Him in the unity of the Holy Spirit.

Mental anguish and emotional suffering accord with the understanding of the person as an amalgam of mental and physical realities together with an emotional awareness which relate to our spiritual existence totally integrated with the physical body. Thus there is a dimension of pain and suffering which can be understood as a loss of this basic physical and spiritual harmony, with the gyroscopic complexities of these complex interdependencies in turmoil to maintain the harmonic status of the whole person.

Thus we could conclude that all pain and suffering are accidents of some form of malfunction or dysfunction understood within the horizons of entropy together with the perfecting process of the evolution of creation towards its perfect state of fulfilment in perfection as created by 'God'.

In the life of Saint Therese we see this hypothetical understanding fulfilled and fulfilling Saint Anselm's teaching that our grasp of the idea of perfection as a proof of the existence of God is indeed manifest in a life ordered to perfection in Christ. For it is clear that Saint Therese grew in the love of God and all humankind. She was inspired to pray and write of her experiences in terms, which though not intended, reveal a life becoming formed in the perfection of the gifts of the Holy Spirit.

The little Saint was enabled to set aside her pain and anguish, her disappointments and her emotional and physical deprivation, and understand her journey of maturing perfection as sometimes enriched and giving greater impetus towards its fulfilment by and with the means of her afflictions. They were not borne in fortitude as a 'stoic' bears them, in blind trust without understanding. Rather they were gathered like flowers to be cut and tended upon and arranged to delight and give succour in contrast to the bland panelling of materialistic existence.

Thus when a gift of a lamb from her father died within a day of her receiving it, she reflected at the burying of this innocent creature, how all things pass away from our possession. Contemplating upon the lamb as if asleep in innocent simple peace, she was moved at her loss but became closer to God. For although she was only a very young child she wrote movingly that this loss brought her closer to her loving God, who draws all things to Him where in that perfection there is no possibility of pain, loss or suffering. She came close to God in her understanding of the truth that all material things pass away and was drawn then to understand to love the gift of her Father as a gift from God, which in the lamb revealed the reality of God the giver. She reflected as her Father dug the grave for his gift and God's gift given to his daughter which was now buried to enrich the good soil of God's creation. In the essence of truth which Saint Therese ever sought the blessing of giver and gift and the gift of blessing by the giver and the gift itself nourished the human heart. She began to learn of the truth that we only possess God in a loving everlasting spiritual embrace and then have any possessions. For all in all with God we will possess all things. For all things were created by Him and are returning to Him. As Saint Aquinas came to understand and know, "All else is straw".

Saint Therese came to know physical pain and suffering as part of a maturing process of total love, a process of sanctification of her life of growth of, and fulfilment in, a spiritual flowering. Her life would be a seedbed of the heart; as the flower fades it is transformed in the seed of the Word of God; coming to fullness through a holy life and death. Thus the channels of grace within her were flooded with transforming action of His Word operative and active as the gift of our all powerful and loving God. The truth of 'God's love' gave purpose to every moment of her life. Pain and suffering were transformed into an intimate sharing in the life of Jesus the Christ. In his sensitive human life and existence He suffered all the frailties of mortality as Immortal God. In this spiritual awareness Therese not only loved in the sense of human love, she loved in Truth with great spiritual intensity and integrity. Jesus Christ true God and man. In this Truth she lived in Truth and that Truth is not only witnessed in her odour of sanctity, but also in the Truth that through her His grace was made manifest in the miracles that flow on to this day.

This purposeful understanding of pain and suffering is of course common to all humankind. A young child often suffers great pain whilst teething and this we accept as an unwanted but acceptable antecedent event to the growing of teeth. This purposeful ability to cope is also there in a woman's acceptance of pain during childbirth and the 'punishing' training regime of a professional athlete. In this understanding and practice, pain is accepted and celebrated as herald to a state of fulfilment, which may lead to a glowing state of heightened sensitivity.

Pain then, may be the herald of good news and the

warning signal of mortal danger. We feel the heat and avoid the fiery furnace. However, St Therese did not suffer for her love. She suffered instead of her Lover, lest He should suffer. She sought to comfort God in His suffering at the perverseness of this human world. She understood physically, emotionally, intellectually and spiritually, the rational consequence of knowing that God loved the world through all the suffering and decay and death that there could ever be. She knew that such a divine and human love of Jesus, true God, second person of the indivisible Trinity, was so great that those who truly loved Him would strive with all their power to comfort Him by sharing, and indeed, experiencing that suffering as a shield and balm of human love, as a truly spiritual embrace and soothing caress.

St Therese sought not to indulge herself or satiate her pleasure; in contrast she sought, out of God's eternal love for her, to return His love and make the heat of desire an instrument not of longing but of peace, as one who already dwelt in the divine presence.

What is life but pain and suffering caused by the accident of creation coming to its perfection through the free will of man, the Son of Man, Jesus the Christ? Accident, human design and disease, this is our portion when we know and love only this world; from this horizon, they are indeed pointless and without purpose.

We are then guided back to the idea and understanding of purpose. The question 'Why?' rings out loud and clear. Why this waste? Why this agony without purpose? Why, when they had so much to live for? Why should this happen to me? To them? To us? Or at all? From the limited horizon of atheistic materialism of the modern belief that nothing really matters or makes sense, then all this suffering, loss and affliction is indeed without purpose. It is all a matter of blind chance and necessity!

However, these questions from the scientific, materialistic enquirer who seeks rational truth, brings with the question 'Why?' and the feeble explanation of chance and necessity, an assumption and grasp of a state of perfection, of order well ordered, ever in balance and harmony, which we know only as a set of transient states of awareness and existence. For pain and suffering are known to us only as the negation of tranquillity and sanguinity, the known state yet unrealised of perfection. These questions of despair assume an understanding and knowledge of human life as it could and should be. Free from all pain and purposeless suffering, free from death and its anguish and suffering to those who remain alive. The assumption is of life as a process or the process for all things to perfection. This assumption is ancillary to St Anselm's proof of the existence of God. For when we posit the perfect, we come self-evidently to the knowledge of a transcendent order of existence, and being omniscient, omnipotent and ever present, as an ordered being and existence eternal and, therefore, prior to creation, then we can assume that there is indeed a loving God Creator of all things.

St Therese, in faith, with hope and in love, of being with her Beloved, as His beloved through death, could and did anticipate the ending of her mortal life of pain and suffering, in tranquillity and sanguine joy.

The Saint's living experiment of life as a process to perfection demonstrates for us the scientific proof that sanctification sought through the cultivation of our spiritual, eternal existence, over and against the limited horizon of our mortal existence, as a life of action carried through in accordance with the Scriptures, Revelation and, in its fullest sense, the tradition of the Universal Church, confirms the assumption. To become fully human as an individual, fulfilled in a life's work which creates out of the seeming frailty of death, an understanding of life, that its significance is the cultivation of harmony between the Spiritual senses and the carnal world of the physical senses, demonstrates, in St Therese's life's work, the verisimilitude of this 'Way of Life', as that which will bring from this individual, action, harmony and peace in all human dealings in this world. For the pattern and reality of her life is within the capacity of many.

The peace and harmony which St Therese brought with her, through her actions and existence in her community, are sure proof that her life's moral and spiritual foundation and fortress of her heart are valid as a Way of Life for all.

It is perverse and unscientific to contemplate and understand such a life, in demonstration of the Christian Way, and declare it 'this way' as non-proven or invalid. It is a scientific demonstration that the underlying and pivotal assumption, through which it was lived and realised, is the proven basis on which all humankind should build and commit their lives.

St Therese at work presents toil and weariness, pain and exhaustion, as an athlete approaches training. It is the necessary exercise of the body and mind to achieve the necessary levels of skills and endurance for excellence of performance.

St Therese trained for excellence in the performance of the eleventh commandment of Jesus. His command to 'love one another as I have loved you' is the way that all followers of Jesus must take. It is a counsel and command for the achievement of perfection. For He was perfect and His command "love one another as I have loved you" sets the standard and commands us to follow. The performance of this command requires us to love unconditionally and, as He demonstrated in His life, this must begin with the denial of 'self-absorption' as the fulcrum of our behaviour in contrast to seeking the comfort and wellbeing of others as the imperative drive to action. Thus St Therese set aside her own comfort and needs as an act of obedience in the Love of Jesus, and sought not only to comfort and bring joy to her friends and acquaintances, but also to comfort Jesus, Himself, and bring joy to Him.

In this matrix of love with friends and with Jesus, pain and suffering became a training regime whereby the objects of love are the singular focus of human fulfilment both physical and spiritual. The person, as an object of love, is the singular focus of attention and action and the Lover, as the Beloved of Jesus, becomes fully human, a lover of all good things.

St Therese sought, as all lovers do, 'the truth', for love seeks perfection and, in perfection, there is truth. Spiritual and bodily perfection in action encompass and encounter suffering, pain and evil, and in this young person's life, her love extended in its effects, far beyond her family and community. Her loving actions reached a world-wide public, for she heals and comforts from beyond the grave, just as she healed and comforted many in her short lifetime. She brings back the stray and confirms the wanderer on their return. She is a missionary, bringing good news to the poor, the message of her Beloved, Jesus the Christ.

The Song of Songs, confirmed in her life, as the Way of Love.

SAINT THERESE

Creation with its roses, the singing stars and the frozen landscapes
of the poles
Is the battlefield where death stalks in the damp, dark depths.
Locked in the embrace of the living God,
Life enspirited is the still peace of creation.
Life in Christ renewing and raising up the dead for creative living.
Living love that marches in triumph with humankind's frustration.
Battlefields are proscribed arenas where life and death are locked in
the combat of survival.
If death survives, then silent chaos will envelop all the planets and
the stars.
From this nothingness God created man in His Universe and made
it good, (therefore)
Death is banished and the order of His goodness prevails over all.
For the resurrection of life embodied in Christ our Saviour is the
way of life, Triumphant throughout the Universe.
It is a cosmic thing like the natural laws of physics.
His resurrection does not need the eye of faith.
It was witnessed and registered on the nerve of human optics.
The wounds He died of were plainly marked in healing.

The scarred hands and feet and back etched out His pain-filled offering.
God as man-made flesh, the conqueror!
Born, like Adam, without sin, He would have lived forever.
This evil world took His life and saluted empire!
From this savage act of brutal waste God wrought Salvation!
Salvation of the Universe governed by His natural laws.
Salvation to humankind made in His image and likeness.
Salvation for all things enspirited, living love our hearts made righteous.
We inhabit creation like a tent and take it with us to the judgement seat.
What have you done? This softly spoken charge will cleave our hearts.
For His wonders and His works, He gave to men and came among us that we could Carry out this charge and hand them back in the beauty of Created Glory.
This is the Paradise, which He wills to share with them.
In freedom we have the will to come to Him
Or, like Adam, we can reach out and fall
In seeking absolute autonomy, as Lord of All.
For God ordained us for His love alone.
A living love in which you will be as one with Him,
Restored in His image and His likeness our heartbeats' tune.
He reveals His laws of physics that we should know
A little of the Glory of His home.

BWF

Contents

Chapter 1

The Vocation of Love
in the Sacred Heart

WE HAVE NOT BEEN 'ADOPTED', THAT IS to say brought in and nurtured, loved and cherished; for all creation has been brought in and nurtured and cherished. We are begotten of God and have, therefore, received the 'Spirit of Adoption'!

In the unity of God, through the Holy Spirit, the advocate in our hearts, we have received the Spirit of Adoption. We did not ask or welcome this divine gift; we receive it in, through and with Christ.

> **Romans 8: 14–17** *We received the spirit of adoption through the Holy Spirit joining Himself with our spirit. We are then enabled to join with the Holy Spirit and exclaim "Abba, Father!" The Holy Spirit bears witness with us that we are 'children of God'.*

The Spirit of Adoption is a change of order in relationship, substance of identity and the character and nature of our

1

existence. For we become, in the Spirit of Adoption, heirs of God, joint heirs with Christ, sharing in His suffering as we share in His Glory.

Christ was adopted into the human race by His earthly father, Saint Joseph; thus He became heir of David, given His name, 'God saves', the Lamb of God who takes away our sins, the Davidic Messiah! As Holy Scripture reveals!

All creation is the beloved servant of God doing His bidding, fulfilling the functions of His natural laws. By contrast, in the freedom of His love through Christ in the Holy Spirit, we are children and heirs to the Kingdom of God.

In the Spirit of Adoption we pray, first giving Glory to God, in thanksgiving to God, in confession to God, in asking to be forever with God and glorifying God in the Spirit. We pray as children of God, heirs with Christ to the Kingdom, as Spiritual exiles co-operating in the redemption and salvation of the Universe.

Thus the Doxology, 'Through Him, with Him, in Him, in the unity of the Holy Spirit, all honour and glory is yours Almighty Father', embraces us in the Spirit of Adoption to which the prayer of witness is adjoined and addressed. For we respond with the great 'Amen!' It is the truth, revealed to us in the Spirit and revealed in us as love's response to the truth. For in our Amen, we have joined in the Spirit of Adoption, the entire prayer of the Mass. We celebrate with the Priest, presiding in Christ, in the saving act of Eucharist.

Prayer then, comes to us in the Holy Spirit and invokes in us our co-labour as children of God and co-heirs with Christ, the chord of truth. Such is prayer of, in and from the heart. A voice rejoicing from our immortal selves that sings in joy, the truth of salvation in His coming.

Prayer wells up like living water; it cascades through the

action of our daily living. It is a well of hope that never fails to quench our thirst. It is a river, cool and refreshing, where we rest and sing the songs of exile. Prayer is His command keeping us safe from the rocks of despair. Prayer is like rain and dappled sunlight in spring. It washes and cleans us and makes us grow strong. Prayer is our guide in the gloom of the chasm, it is our sandal and staff and light in the darkness. For prayer is the order of perfection acknowledged, of God here with us, God present before us and God transcendent, beyond us.

His call is our prayer. Our response to His calling through His Word is demonstrated in the beauty of His coming. Let our lives be a prayer and our death be His triumph, for in living in Him, all is possible.

As incense, may our prayers rise like perfumed aromas, an odour of sanctity lifted up to greet Him. From here, in the flesh, He suffered and died, our acceptable offering, united in prayer, united in suffering; He arose from the dead, the prayer of salvation, united in Him. The Holy Spirit joins us in rejoicing, for the Lamb is worthy, all our hope is in Him!

Thus the pathway of prayer is the structure of hearts where, in our spirit of life, the Holy Spirit abides. Prayer in the Christian way of life is our understanding of the revelation of God immanent, the third person of the Holy Trinity, sent into our hearts by God incarnate, at the right hand in Glory, with the Father. Prayer flows like the current of an electric field, the dynamo of our Spiritual selves. Prayer is the current of grace flowing from creation's holiness. God created all things good. As the Holy One, He creates all things Holy, ordered to His will. As created beings, our very existence is prayer, contorted by material decay, which through man's inordinate desire for immortality and power over life and death leads us to seek power through death and its coercive dread.

Prayer is not an antidote or balm; it is the voice of holiness within us calling us to order our lives to the will of God.

The goal and reward of prayer is a holy life in Christ, in the unity of the Holy Spirit. All existence in the Universe is ordered to it. This truism of prayer is ignored by the world. Distracted by its beauty, the materialist knows only material things and does not even pause to wonder at the nature of that immaterial thing, beauty of itself!

Beauty, as the right and perfect ordering of things, speaks openly and distinctly of the perfection of the Creator. For in that intricate, many-layered facet of its ordering, there appear many minor horizons of sentient knowing. From history and language, through the material sciences, to the philosophy of Revelation, there is a university of knowing which is our true inheritance in understanding. All known in their beauty that draws man on to a wider, deeper, more refined understanding of the nature of creation.

Prayer, however, is not part of sentient knowing. Prayer, in part, expresses the unconfined joy in our existence. Existence not confined by material nature, but in that existence of our imaging, which knows and engages reality as an abstract of perfection.

From this abstract, fountains the creative brushstroke where the fingers of the heart and hand and eye reach out to the blank face of the canvas and from the pigment dust, fashion beauty and things inconsequent and their history. There is a thrill of wonder when we stand before the beautiful. The profound depiction of the poor in agony in perfection has its own ordering of the beautiful. For here, prayer is holiness transforming all to the perfection of life in Jesus the Christ arisen. When He arose, the waste and stench of death's decay from life was ordered to His perfect holiness. The material, created Universe was realigned to goodness and the will of God, for as God made man, the Universe is at one in His existence evolving to its climax in His second coming.

The judgement of the perfect, of our offering – the poor and lame, the weak and lowly will not be changed but rather perfected in sentient unity. For there is no hierarchy in perfection, just a balanced compass of harmonies in which exists immortal beauty.

> *Pray then with Saint Therese that the little way of Two Thousand years of love Will appear before Him as a rose bowl offering. May our poverty and brokenness be a prayer for Him. Our broken hearts and wayward wills, a ring for Him, a sign in the witness of our Confession of our love for Him.*
>
> *Father, we see your Glory and Hallow your name. Let the child, Jesus, be our Champion. Let the smile of Mary be our gift offering. Let the Lamb of God at rest be our remembering. Let our prayer be our pain and loss and suffering. For we suffer naught that suffer here, at one with Him.*
>
> *Saint Therese, take charge of our hearts for the Third Millennium. The Sacred Heart, heart of His Church, take all into the fire of your love. Saint Joseph, take our hand and walk with us. Let us, as sisters and brothers of Jesus, be at home with you and Mary in the house of Nazareth.*
>
> *For the little way of love is the family at peace in your home, the home of Our Father, who is in heaven.*
>
> *BWF*

BROTHER OF SAINT FRANCIS
LAMB OF ST THERESE

Saint Therese, Mission of the Sacred Heart of His mystical Body, the Church

'The Way', is Christ's way, it is His way; it is His word, His prayer, His teaching, His promises, His commands.

We are followers of His way, of no other way. It is the little way of love along the King's highway, the pathway into His Kingdom – His Kingdom with His Father, Our Father who is in heaven. This is the little way of Saint Therese of Lisieux.

The flowering, meadow tapestry of this way of Christ is the Canticle of Canticles, the Song of Songs – the great love epic of the Beloved of the Old Testament – fulfilled in Christ, completed by 'the Word made flesh who dwells among us'.

The Gospels, the New Testament, are the fulfilment of Salvific history. They reveal, in Therese, the great signs of true devotion and adoration and reveal the truth of all things in the holiness of His love which sets fire to the Saint's heart – the fire of adoration which burns forever. For like the burning bush, Saint Therese, through the love of God, became a sign of His love and a Doctor of His Universal Church, the ever enduring sign of all consuming love – 'the Word made flesh that dwells here with us'!

Let us recall the Word in the **Gospel of Luke**, chapter two, verses forty-one to fifty:

Every year His parents used to go to Jerusalem for the feast of the Passover. When He was twelve years old, they went up for the feast as usual. When the days of the feast were over, they set off home. The little boy Jesus stayed behind in Jerusalem without His parents becoming aware of His sojourn. They thought that Jesus was with them in the caravan party, but at the end of the first day's journey, they failed to find Him among their friends and acquaintances. They hurried back to Jerusalem looking for Him everywhere.

The Son of God, Son of Man, a child of twelve was missing! His mother and Joseph, His adopted father, were distraught, anxious that their precious son, their charge from God was missing, lost. This teaches us something of the awesome responsibility of trust that God the Father laid upon His human parents, Mary and Joseph.

'Saint Joseph and Mary, the Mother of God, you nourished and cared for Jesus, Son of Man, Son of God. Watch over us and protect us with Saint Therese on our journey to Our Father.'

It took them three days before they found Him in the Temple, sitting amongst the scribes and Sadducees. He was listening to them and enquiring of them. All those who heard Him were astounded at His intelligence and the wisdom in His replies. Saint Joseph and Mary were overcome when they saw Him, and His mother said to Him, "My child, why have you done this to us? See how worried your father and I have been as we looked for you."

He replied, "Why were you looking for me? Did you not know that you would find me in my Father's House? I must be in my Father's House!" They did not fully understand what Jesus meant.

Thus Jesus teaches that He is Son of Man, Son of God, dwelling in His Father's house. This He fulfilled at the Last Supper when He consecrated the bread and wine as His Body and Blood. He would then be present always in us, His

Church, in Him, through His Holy Spirit, and therefore, we will join Him in Eucharist where He is, in His Father's house.

A Canticle of Love addressed to the Saint's sister, her eldest sister Marie – Sister Mary of the Sacred Heart.

My beloved sister, you have asked me to leave you some token and now that I have our Mother's permission, I am glad to talk awhile with you! (You, who are doubly my sister; with you who lent me your voice when I could not speak, promising in my name that I would serve Jesus only.) The child who writes these lines tonight, dear godmother, is the child whom you offered to the Lord and who loves you as a child loves its mother. Only in Heaven will you be able to fathom the depth of gratitude that fills my heart.

You wish to learn the secrets which Jesus confides to your godchild and yet you know these secrets for they are already yours. For it was you who taught me to listen to His teaching.

> **Meditate.** *The Saint's secrets of devotion and holiness are the teaching of Jesus. This lesson of devoted listening to the Word of God is her legacy to us, for we are the children of Jesus, of St Therese of Filton.*

The Saint continues:

I will try to tell you something, although I am only too conscious of the impossibility of the capacity of human speech to put into words what the heart itself can scarcely grasp.

Do not think I am overwhelmed with consolations. Far from it! My joy consists in being deprived of all earthly joys. Jesus does not guide me openly; I do not see Him or hear Him. Nor is it through books that I learn, for often I do not understand what I am reading.

Yet sometimes, I am consoled by choice words, such as the following, which I read this evening after my meditation passed away into utter dryness:

"Here is the Master I give thee. He will teach you all that you should do. I will to make you read in the Book of Life, wherein you will find the 'science of love'."

(These words were spoken by Our Lord to Saint Margaret Mary.)

'The science of love'; how sweetly do these words re-echo in my soul! I want for no other knowledge and like the Beloved in the *Canticle of Canticles*, 'having given away all the substance of my house, for love, I reckon it (the substance of myself) as nothing'.

> **Song of Songs 8: 7** *Love no flood can quench nor torrents drown. Were a man to offer all his family wealth to purchase love contempt is all that he would gain.*

I understand clearly that through love only can we become pleasing to God and my sole ambition is to acquire it. Jesus condescends to give me the knowledge that the only way which leads to love's divine furnace is the way of self-surrender. This self-surrender is like the confidence of the little child who sleeps without any trace of apprehension or fear in its Father's arms.

Through the mouth of the author, the Holy Ghost has said:

> **Proverbs 9: 4 whoever is a little one, let him come unto me.**

And elsewhere the same Spirit of Love declares that:

> **Wisdom. 6: 7** *To him that is little, mercy is granted.*

In His name also, the Prophet Isaiah reveals how, on the last day, the Lord:

> **Isaiah. 40: 11** *shall feed His flock like a shepherd. He shall gather together the lambs in His arms and hold them close to His bosom and lead to their rest the mother ewes.*

As if these proofs were insufficient, the same Prophet, whose inspired gaze penetrated the depths of eternity, cried out:

> **Isaiah. 66: 13** *Thus saith the Lord: "you will be suckled at the breast, carried on her hip and fondled in her lap. As a mother comforts a child, so shall I comfort you. You will be comforted in Jerusalem."*

O, my beloved sister, after hearing such words, one can only be silent and weep, weep for love. If all weak and imperfect souls such as mine, felt as I do, none would despair of reaching the summit of the mountain of love, since Jesus does not look for deeds, but only for gratitude and self-surrender.

Does He not say in the Prayers of the Church:

> **Psalms. 50: 9-15** *I will not accept any bull from your homes nor a single goat from your folds. For all forest creatures are mine already; the animals on their mountains, in their thousands. I know every bird of*

10

the air. Whatever moves in the fields is mine. If I am
hungry, I shall not tell you Since the world and all it
holds is mine Am I to eat the flesh of bulls? And drink
the blood of goats?

Let thanksgiving be your sacrifice to God, fulfil
the vows you make to the most high. Then, if you call
me in time of trouble, I will rescue you and you will
honour me.

"This is all that God claims of us. He needs our love; he has no need of our works. True this is the same God who declares that He has no need to tell us if he be hungry. Yet he did not disdain to ask a little water from the Samaritan woman. When He said 'give me a drink' He, the creator was asking for the love of his creatures. He thirsted indeed but He thirsted for love. Our Divine Lord's thirst is more intense than it ever was. Among the disciples of this world, He meets with nothing but indifference and ingratitude. Among His own how few are the hearts that surrender themselves without reserve to the infinite tenderness of His love!"

"Happy indeed are we who are privileged to understand the intimate secrets of our Divine spouse. If you would set down in writing all you know what beautiful pages would be given for us to read. You prefer however to keep the secrets of the King hidden in your heart. To me you say 'it is honourable to reveal and confess the works of God', yet I think you do well to keep silent for no words on earth can communicate the secrets of heaven."

Meditate
Tobit 12:1 – 21.

11

"As for me after writing page upon page I should feel that I had not yet begun. So varied is the outlook of so infinite coloured variations. That the palette of the Divine painter would alone be able when the night of this life has passed, to supply me with the colours needed to portray the wonders which my soul catches sight of, glimpses of the beauty in the luminous presence of His Love."

"Since however my dearest sister you have expressed the wish to penetrate into the sanctuary of my heart and have in writing an account of the most consoling dream of my life together with my 'Little Doctrine' as you call it I will comply with that wish in the following pages. I will address myself to the Lord (this is the pattern of The Canticle) for by so doing I will be better able to set down my thoughts. You may find my expressions somewhat exaggerated but I assure you there is no exaggeration in my heart, there is only peace and calm."

"My Jesus how gently and tenderly do you lead my soul."

"The storm has raged in me since Easter the Glorious feast of your Triumph, until in the month of May, there shone through the darkness of my night one clear ray of your grace."

"While dwelling on the mysterious dreams which you send sometimes to your favoured ones. I thought that such dreams were not for me for in my soul it was always darkest night. Then I fell asleep amidst the fury of the storm. The following morning May 10th, at the first glimmer of dawn I dreamt I was walking alone in a gallery with our mother. When suddenly without understanding how they had entered, I saw three Carmelites wearing their mantles and long veils. I knew they came from heaven and I thought how glad I would be if I could only see the face of one of them. As if my wish had been heard the tallest of the three Saints advanced towards me. I fell upon my knees and an inexpressible joy took possession of me as she raised her veil or rather threw it around me."

"Without a moment's hesitation I recognised our venerable mother Anne of Jesus, foundress of the Carmel in France. Her face was an unearthly beauty, no rays came from it yet in spite of the thick veil that enveloped us I could see it was suffused with a soft light which seemed to emanate from her. She caressed me most tenderly and finding myself the object of such affection. I took courage to say 'dear mother I implore you to tell me, will Our Lord leave me much longer in this world?'"

'Will He not come to fetch me?' Smiling sweetly, she answered me, 'Yes, soon, very soon, I promise you.' 'Dear Mother,' I asked again, 'does He want more from me than these poor little acts and desires that I offer Him? Is He pleased with me?' Our Venerable Mother's face then shone with fresh splendour and her expression became indescribably more gracious and she answered, 'God asks nothing more of you, He is pleased, very much pleased.' Then she took my head between her hands and she kissed me so lovingly that nothing in language can convey the sweetness of her embrace. My heart was full of joy and recalling my sisters, I was about to beg some favour for them when, alas, I awoke."

"I cannot express the happiness that filled my being. Months have now passed since this wonderful dream, yet in recall, it has lost nothing of its freshness and heavenly sanctity. I see the loving faces of the holy Carmelites and feel the fondness of her caress". "Jesus, you commanded the stillness of the wind and rainstorm and there came deep calm." **(Matthew. 8: 26)**

We meditate on the Saint's teaching of the universal nature of human life. Part of His creation, the storm in our hearts and minds is calmed just as He calms the raging tempest or the oceans. He is the universal Lord who, because we are all precious to Him, receiving the balm of His word, the anointing of Saving Justice, through the gracious love of Jesus the Christ, His only Son.

Blessed be God forever.

"On waking, I realised that heaven does exist, a heaven peopled and alive with those who cherish me as their child."

> **Meditate.** *Let us meditate upon the Saint's knowledge of heaven. It is a place peopled, thronged with those who cherish us as children of God. Let the mighty be humbled for they must come as little children to be cradled and cherished in the Kingdom of heaven. We must come out of love like little children, for that is precisely what we are, no more and no less – children of God, brothers and sisters of Jesus, Our Lord and Saviour.*

The Saint says, "This impression still remains and is sweeter yet, because up to that time, I had no devotion to the Venerable Mother Anne of Jesus. I had never sought her help, nor thought of her unless I heard her name which is seldom. Now I know how constantly she held me in her presence. This makes my love grow and widen out, not only for her, but for all in my Father's House.

14

"My Beloved, this was a prelude to yet greater graces which you poured out upon me. Let me remind them of you today and forgive my silliness if I tell you once more of my longings and hopes that reach out to border on the infinite. Forgive me, that my soul may be healed. Do you, I beseech thee, fulfil all its desires."

> **Meditate.** *We too, ask for forgiveness of Our Lord Jesus, the Christ. We humbly ask for healing and that our souls, in the purity of your creation, should be fulfilled in all their desires in you, Our Saviour, Jesus Christ.*

"To be thy spouse, O my Jesus, to be a daughter of Carmel and, through my union with you, be the mother of souls. Should not this content me? Yet other vocations make themselves apparent and I would wield the sword, I would be a priest, an apostle, a martyr, a Doctor of the Church. I long to accomplish the most heroic deeds, the spirit of the crusader burns within me and I would gladly die upon the battlefield in defence of the Church."

> **Meditate.** *Lift us up, Lord, in the loving desires of our hearts. Let holy fervour consume us as it consumed Saint Therese. This fervour of love is the love of the Father for the Son, through the Holy Spirit burning in our hearts.*

"The vocation of the Priesthood! With what love, my Jesus, would I bear thee in my hand when my words brought thee down from heaven! With what love too, would I give thee to the faithful! With all my longing to be a priest, I admire and envy the humility of St Francis of Assisi and feel myself drawn to imitate him by refusing that divine dignity. How can I reconcile these opposite desires?"

"Like the prophets and the doctors, I would be a light unto their souls. I would travel the world over to preach thy name, O my Beloved, to raise on heathen soil, the standard of the Cross. One mission alone would not satisfy my longings. I would spread the Gospel in all points of the earth, even the farthest islands. I would be a missionary, not for a few years only. Were it possible, I should desire it to have been from the world's creation and to remain one until the end of time. The greatest of all my desires is to win the martyr's palm. Martyrdom was the dream of my youth and the dream has grown more vivid in Carmel's narrow cell. Yet this, too, is folly, since to satisfy my thirst for suffering, not one, but every kind of torture would be needful."

"Like thee, my adorable spouse, I would be scourged, I would be crucified! I would be flayed like Bartholomew, plunged into boiling oil like St John and like St Ignatius of Antioch, ground by the teeth of wild beasts into a bread worthy of God."

> **Meditate.** *The bread of heaven is food for our souls, real bread; spiritual bread consecrated in Jesus the Christ's life of suffering which forms the new and everlasting covenant which, with St Therese, we offer at the Mass. It is bread, the Body of Christ, which in its perfection, perfects us and is the offering acceptable to God for the salvation of the world.*

The Saint continues: "With St Agnes and St Cecilia, I would offer my neck to the sword of the executioner and with Joan of Arc, murmur the name of Jesus at the burning stake. When I ponder on the fearful torments awaiting Christians at the time of Anti Christ; my heart pounds within me and I desire that these torments could be reserved for me. Open Jesus, the Book of Life in which are written the deeds of your Saints. Each one of these deeds I long to accomplish for you!"

"To folly such as this, what answer will thou give to me? Is there on earth a soul more feeble than mine? Yet precisely out of my feebleness, you have been delighted to grant my least, my most childlike desires and now you will to realise those other accomplishments more vast than the whole Universe."

> **Meditate.** *O Lord, far greater than the folly of our most fabulous longings, your will to wrought in your saints the most perfect of offerings, the deepest of humility of the Incarnation. God in His majesty reduced to the weakness of human flesh. Lord, perfect us in this humbleness, let us come to you as children of your love – your love returning as beloved to the bosom of love. We ask Jesus, the Word, to dwell in our senses and, thus illumined, join in the loving goodness of the Holy Spirit alive in our hearts, that we can rise, children of the light, to walk humbly with God who wills the goodness of perfection for all.*
> **Alleluia, Alleluia.**

"These aspirations becoming a real martyrdom, I one day sought relief in the Epistles of Saint Paul and my eyes opened as I read the 12th and 13th chapters of the first of the Epistles to the Corinthians. There, on the second page, I read that all cannot become apostles, prophets or doctors. The Church is composed of different members – the eye cannot function as the hand. The answer was clear but it neither satisfied my longing nor brought me the peace I sought.

"Then descending into the interior depths of my nothingness, I was so lifted up that I reached my desired goal."

[Here the Saint is following the teaching of St John of the Cross.]

"Without being discouraged, I read on and found great comfort in the counsel: 'Be zealous in desiring the better gifts, you will be shown a more excellent way.'" **(1 Corinthians. 12: 31)**

"The Apostle then explains how all the better gifts are nothing without love and that Charity is the most excellent way of going in safety to God. At last I had found rest!"

"'Though I command languages both human and Angelic, if I speak without love, I am no more than a gong booming or a cymbal clashing'." **(1 Corinthians. 13: 1)**

The Saint now lays before us her illumination as she meditated on the mystical body of Holy Church.

At last, she had found rest in the Hymn of Love of Saint Paul.

"As I meditated on the mystical Body of Holy Church, I could not recognise myself among any of its members described by St Paul. I came to know that I desired to recognise myself in all. Charity gave me the key to the revelation of 'my vocation'. I understood that since the Church is a body composed of differing members, she could not lack the most necessary and that which she is most nobly endowed of all bodily organs. I understood therefore, that the Church has a heart in the Scriptural sense, a heart on fire with love.

I saw too, that love alone imparts life to all members, so that should love ever fail, apostles would no longer preach the Gospel and martyrs would avoid shedding their blood.

Finally, I realised that love includes every vocation, that love is all things; that love is eternal, reaching out through the ages and reaching out to the utmost limits of the Universe."

> **Meditate.** *Through this Saint, most cherished, the vocation to the laity is opened wide, from the enclosed life of Carmel comes the message of the loving vocation to us, the laity, unenclosed except by the Mystical Body of Christ, His Church.*

"The vocation of Love in the Sacred Heart."

"Beside myself with joy, I cried out, exultant in my heart and soul, 'O Jesus, my Love, my vocation is found at last, My Vocation is Love.' 'I have found my place in the bosom of the Church and this place, O my God. You have yourself, given to me, in the heart of the Church, my Mother, I will be Love. Thus I shall be, all things, and my dream will be fulfilled. Why do I say 'beside myself with joy', when it is rather, peace that has become my portion, the calm, quiet peace of the sailor as he catches sight of the beacon which guides him to port?'"

"O luminous beacon of love! I know how to reach even into the heart of your fire. I have found the secret of making them my own."

1 Corinthians. 13 *If I speak, let it be with love. If I have the gift of knowledge, let me pass it on with love. In love, let my faith make me grow to God. Let my giving be out of love.May my fasting be an act of love. From love may patience blossom and kindness grow. Love, drive away jealousy, boastfulness and conceit. Love, drive away my self-seeking and rudeness. Love, make me ever forgiving, set me against all wrongdoing. Love, let me rejoice in Truth with compassion for all. To trust, to hope, to endure whatever comes This is the 'Little Way of Love.'*

Chapter 2

Love is Exchanged
for Love Alone

WE CONTINUE TO LISTEN TO SAINT THERESE as she writes to her sister in the Carmel at Lisieux an account of her vocation and her 'little doctrine'. We are then reminded of the Beatitudes.

Matthew. 5: 1–3 *Seeing the crowds, He went onto the mountain. When He was seated His disciples came to Him. Then He began to speak and this is what He taught:*

'Blessed indeed are the poor in spirit, the Kingdom of heaven is theirs.'

'Blessed are the poor in spirit', this poverty goes hand in hand with the spiritual childhood necessary for us to enter into the Kingdom of heaven.

Meditate. *Blessed are the gentle, the unassuming, who have no demands except the desire to give, for we are His creatures and, in His love, let us return to Him* *for we have only ourselves to give out of love, as His Beloved.*

Psalms. 37: 34 *Put your hope in Yahweh, keep to His path. He will raise you up to make the land your own; you will look on while the wicked are banished.* ***Amen.***

St Therese writes to her sister for us: "I am but a weak and helpless child and it is my weakness which makes me able to dare offer myself, O Jesus, as victim of your love. During the time of the Old Testament, only pure and spotless holocausts were acceptable to the Omnipotent God. His justice in the 'wrath of mercy' could not be appeased except by the perfect sacrifice."

"Now that the law of fear [Torah] has given way to the 'law of love', I have been chosen, although I am a weak and imperfect creature, Love's victim. This is surely a fitting choice, for in order that Love may be wholly satisfied, it must reduce itself to nothingness and that nothingness in the sight of love is transformed in the Holy fire of His Love."

Love is exchanged for love alone.

This is Saint Therese's motto inspired by the teaching of Saint John of the Cross. 'My God, this I know most fully. Therefore, I have striven and found a way to ease my heart by giving you "love for your love".'

Luke 16: 9 *Use the spoilt riches of this world to make yourself friends who will welcome you into* *eternal dwellings. For the children of this world are more astute in dealing with their own kind than the children of the Light. This is the advice Jesus gave to His disciples.*

Saint Therese continues :"I was a child of light and I understood that my desires of being all things, embracing every vocation, were riches that might well spoil me and make me unjust, so I employed them in the making of friends. Mindful of the prayerful request of Elisha when he asked the prophet Elijah for a double share of his spirit, I presented myself before the company of Angels and the Saints and I addressed them with these words: 'I am the least of all creatures, I know my worthlessness, I also know that noble and generous hearts love to do good. Therefore, Blessed inhabitants of the Heavenly City, I ask you to adopt me as your child. All the glory you may help me to acquire will be yours. Accept then to hear my prayer and obtain for me a double portion of your Love for God.'"

> **Meditate.** *We lift up our hearts and minds to heaven and to the Angels and Saints who inhabit the heavenly Kingdom. May we, followers of the 'Little Flower', echo her prayer, her entreaty, and ask for us a portion of your love for God. We ask this in the name of Saint Therese, through our Beloved Jesus the Christ and His Prophet Elijah. In the Jordan of your Baptism we join the Angels and Saints in singing the praises of the Holy One. For it was then that the heavens opened and the Beloved Son was revealed to us.*

Saint Therese continues: "I dare not try to understand all that my prayer means, O my God. I tremble before the weight and magnificence of its audacious request. My plea is that I am your child; in this I am not culpable for children do not grasp the full and most profound understanding of their words. Yet, if parents acquired the means, by mounting a throne or inheriting great wealth, they would not hesitate in granting the desires of the little ones who are dearer to them than life itself. To please them, they would give most lavishly, inclining their care and compassion to weakness, the indulgence of generous love."

"Now the Church is a Queen because she is your spouse, Divine King of Kings. I am a child of Holy Church. I do not ask for riches or glory, not even the glory of heaven. Heaven belongs by right to my brothers and sisters, the Angels and Saints. My own glory will be the reflection of the radiance that streams from the brow of my Mother, the Church. I ask for love."

"From now on, I have just one single motivating thought, dear Jesus, it is to love you! Great deeds are denied to me. I can neither preach the Gospel nor shed my blood, but what does it matter? My brother's labour instead of me whilst I, a little child, stay close to the Throne and love there, in place of all those caught up in the daily combat of this world."

"How can I show, in reality, my love, since love is made manifest in deeds? I, the little one, will strew flowers, perfuming the Divine Throne with their fragrance. I will sing love's canticle in silvery tones. Thus will my short life be spent in thy sights, O my Beloved! To strew flowers is the only means of proving my love and these flowers will be the daily round of each word and look, every little daily sacrifice. I wish to make value out of the smallest actions and do them all for Love. For Love's sake, I want to both suffer and rejoice, so I shall cast my flowers. Not before anyone I can see, but rejoicing all the while, I will scatter these petals before Thee. Should my roses be gathered from the midst of thorns, the sweeter will be my prayerful refrain.

What use to you are my flowers and my songs, dear Jesus, what use are they to you? I know well that this fragrant shower, these petals of little price, these songs of love from this poor little heart of mine, will however be pleasing to you. They are trifles; it is so, yet thou will smile on them.

The Church Triumphant, bending lovingly over her child will gather up these fallen rose leaves and place them into your Divine hands. Then they will acquire infinite value and they will shower down on the Church's suffering to extinguish the flames and they will clothe the Church Militant, in her triumph.

My Jesus, I love you! I love my Mother, the Church. I recall that 'the least act of pure love is of more value to her than all other works combined'. Does this pure love really exist in my heart? Are not my boundless desires, flights of fancy, mere folly? If they are, I beseech you; enlighten me for I seek only the truth. If my longings are too bold, deliver me from them for then they would be the most grievous of all martyrdoms. I confess to you, that should I fail to reach the heights to which my soul aspires, I shall have tasted more sweetness in my martyrdom, in my folly, than I shall taste in eternal bliss. Unless by a miracle, thou take from me all memory of the hopes which I cherished here upon earth. Jesus, Jesus, the desire of your love awakens such delight, what must it be like to possess and enjoy it forever?

How can a soul so imperfect as mine reach up to the

plenitude of your love? What is the key to this mystery? Friend, why do you not reserve these great ambitions for great souls, for eagles who rise up and soar in the heights of holiness? I am an unfledged nestling, yet the eagle's spirit is mine, nor does my frailty prevent me gazing on the Divine Sun of Love. I am on fire to rise upwards into its flames. I long to glide as the eagle does but I can only flap my wings. It is beyond my feeble powers to rise and soar."

> **Meditate.** *Let us pray for the good things made ready for us in heaven, the good things of His love. We are His Beloved just as Therese and His Church are His Beloved. He raises up our hearts in the Holy Spirit where we meet and greet the Son at the right hand of the Father. Let us one day fly to thee, raised up on the updraught of your love. We ask Saint Therese to guide and keep us in your love.*

"What is to become of me? Must I perish in sorrow because of my helplessness? No, I will not even grieve. With foolhardy confidence and reckless of my life, I will remain here till death, my gaze fixed upon the Divine Sun. Nothing can frighten me, neither storm nor flood. Should impenetrable clouds conceal the Orb of Love; should it seem in that eclipse that beyond this life there is only darkness, this would be my hour of perfect joy, the hour when my confidence in you would know no bounds, for knowing that beyond those dark clouds, my Sun is shining. In this inner peace, I should never remove my devoted gaze."

"O my God, although in this way I understand your love for me, you know also how often I lose this vision of my only devotion. I stray from your side and allow my wings to be draggled in the muddy pools of this world. Then 'I cry like a young swallow' **(Isaiah. 38: 14)**, my cry tells you of my distress and you come to me. O, Infinite Mercy, 'you come, not to call the just, but sinners.' **(Matthew. 9: 13)"**

"Yet should you remain deaf to the plaintive cries of your feeble creature. Should you still cover yourself from my sight, I am content to be numb with cold, my wings bedraggled and once more would I rejoice in such well-merited suffering. O Divine Sun, I am happy to feel myself so small and frail in your presence and my heart rests at peace, for I know that all the eagles of your celestial court have pity on me, that they guard and defend me, putting to flight the vultures, the demons that hover near to devour me. I do not fear the evil encroachment of these demons for I am not destined to be their prey, for I am the prey of the Divine Eagle, who watches over and ever protects me."

"Eternal Word, my Saviour, you are the Divine Eagle who seduces me, whom I love. You, who descended to this land of exile, who willed to suffer and die, in order to save each single soul and place it into the very heart of the Most Blessed Trinity, Love's Eternal Home. You, who upon returning to the realm of light, yet remain hidden here in our valley of tears under the form of the white Host, to nourish me with your own substance. Forgive me, Jesus, if I tell you that your love reaches out into insanity, that at the sight of such grand folly that you will, my own heart leaps out of me up to you. How could my trust have any limits?"

> **Meditate.** *We are moved by your love, Lord, to consume you and be consumed in your love. We come*

before you, in the Mass, as little children with our hearts burning with the love of your Sacred Heart in the midst of your mystical body, the Church. Your body is one with your spouse, our Holy Mother. In this Divine Communion, we rest in your embrace. Jesus, we embrace you on the Cross, reaching up to comfort you as we are comforted in your presence.

"I know well that the Saints, for your sake have made themselves foolish, but being 'eagles', they have done great things. I am too feeble for such mighty deeds. My joy lies in the hope that I am accepted into your love as a victim. In this I am confident that the Angels and Saints will help me fly to you, on your wings, O my Divine Eagle. As long as you will that it be so, I shall remain with my gaze fixed upon you, for I long to become a victim of your Love. I am filled with hope that one day you will swoop down upon me and bear me off to the source of all Love, plunging me, at last, into its glowing depths that I may reside forever, its happy victim."

"Jesus, I long to tell all little souls of your humble compassion and ineffable condescension. If it is possible that you could find a little one weaker than me – someone who would abandon himself with perfect trust to your Infinite Mercy, I am certain that you would delight in loading that soul with ever greater favours. Where do these desires come from, O my spouse, to make known the secrets of your Love? It is you alone who have taught them to me and who reveal them to others. I know you can do these things and I beseech thee to do so. I beseech you, Jesus, to glance a look upon a vast number of little souls. I implore you and entreat upon you to choose a legion of little victims of this world, worthy of your love."

June 1894. My song of today

"O, how I love thee, Jesus, my soul aspires to thee and yet, for one day only, my simple prayer I pray. Come reign within my heart, smile tenderly on me Today, Dear Lord, today.

But if I dare take thought of what tomorrow brings, it fills my fickle heart with dreary, dull dismay. I crave, indeed my God, the cross of sufferings but only for today. Sweetest Star of Heaven, Virgin Spotless, Blest Shining with Jesus' light, guiding Him my way. Mother, beneath your veil, let my tired spirit rest For this brief passing day. Soon shall I fly far, among the Holy Choirs. Then shall the joy be mine that knows no decay. Then my lips will sing to heaven's angelic rhymes, The eternal glad tidings of today. Offering myself as a victim to God's Merciful Love."

This prayer was enclosed in the Saint's copy of the Gospels, which she carried night and day next to her heart.

"O, my God, O most Blessed Trinity, I desire both to love thee and to make thee loved; to labour for the Glory of your Church by saving souls here upon earth and by delivering those who are suffering in Purgatory. I desire to fulfil perfectly your will and to reach the degree of Glory you have prepared for me in the Kingdom. In a word, I desire to be Holy, knowing how helpless I am, I plead of you, my God that you, yourself, be my holiness. Since you love me so much that you gave me your only begotten Son to be my Saviour and my spouse, then the infinite treasures of His merits are mine. I offer them gladly to you and I ask you to look upon me through the eyes of Jesus and accept His heart aflame with Love.

In addition to this, I offer you all the merits of the Saints in heaven and on earth, together with their acts of love and those of the Holy Angels. Finally, I offer you, Blessed Trinity, the love and merits of the Blessed Virgin, my dearest Mother. It is to her I commit this oblation, asking her to present it to you. During the days of His life on earth, her divine son, my sweet spouse, spoke these words:

'If you ask my Father anything in my name, He will give it to you.' **(John 16: 23)**

Therefore, I am certain you will grant my prayer. My God, I know that the more you will to bestow, the more do you make us desire these gifts. In my heart I know boundless desires and I confidently ask that you take possession of my soul. I cannot receive you in Holy Communion as often as I desire. You are all powerful. Abide in me as you do in the Tabernacle; never abandon your little victim. I long to console you for ungrateful sinners and I implore you to take away my liberty so that I can cause you no displeasure. If through weakness, I should chance to fall, may a glance from your eyes cleanse my soul in a twinkling and consume all my imperfections as fire transforms all things into itself.

I thank you, O my God, for all the graces you have given me, especially for having purified me in the crucible of suffering. At the day of judgement I shall look with joy upon you, carrying your sceptre of the cross. Because you have given me this precious cross as my portion, I hope to be like you in Paradise and gaze upon the sacred wounds of your Passion as they shine on my glorified body.

After this exile upon earth, I hope to possess you for all eternity but I do not seek to lay up treasures in heaven. I long to labour for your love alone with the sole purpose of pleasing you, to console your Sacred Heart and save souls who will love you through all eternity.

When the evening of life comes, I shall stand before you with empty hands, because I do not ask that you take any account of my works. All our good deeds are tarnished in your sight. Robe me then, in your own Justice so that I may receive from your Love, the everlasting gift of yourself. I long for no other throne, no other crown, but only you, My Beloved. Before your majesty, time holds no sway, 'one day is a thousand years'. **(Psalms. 39: 4)**

You can, in an instant, prepare me for my appearance before you. In order that my life may be one act of perfect love, I offer myself as a holocaust to your Merciful Love. I implore you to consume me in your love without cessation, to allow the floods of your infinite tenderness gathered up in you, to overflow into my soul, that I become a martyr of your love, O my God. May this martyrdom one day release me to appear before you and may my soul, this day, take flight into the eternal embrace of your merciful love.

My Beloved, I desire, at every beat of my heart, to renew this oblation an infinite number of times 'till the shadows retire' **(Song of Songs 4: 6)** and then I can tell you of my love face to face."

Mary, Frances, Therese of the Infant Jesus and the Holy Face.

This ninth day of June,
Feast of the most Holy Trinity
The year of grace 1895.

Morning Offering
(Manuscript at Carfin)

O my God, I offer you all my actions today for the intentions and for the glory of the Sacred Heart of Jesus. I long to sanctify every beat of my heart, my every thought, my simplest works, by uniting them to the infinite merits of your love. I desire to make reparation for my sins by casting them into the furnace of the merciful love of the Sacred Heart.

O my God, I ask you for myself and for all whom I hold dear, the grace to fulfil perfectly your Holy Will; to accept for love of thee, the joys and sorrows of this passing life, that one day we may be united together in heaven for all eternity.

Amen.

Meditate. *The love of God floods into our lives and in Jesus' love we immerse our thoughts and as Saint Therese says, 'each and every heart beats as He wills.'*

Saint Therese, in her prayers, in her work, in her suffering, knew the breath of His love. She longed to look upon the Holy Face and lose herself in His divine gaze.

Saint Therese, you teach us, your little ones, to abandon ourselves in the fire of His love. Hold our hands, Saint Therese, let us dance in the summer meadows of the Father's Kingdom.

We pray on this day for our hearts to be ever

faithful in accord with His will. Guide us, Saint Therese, that our hands be empty but our hearts on fire with His love.

Saint Therese, teach us the Little Way of love.

CHAPTER 3

THE APOSTLE OF PRAYER

IN THE PENULTIMATE AND LAST VERSE OF **John 6**, leading us into the Prayer of Jesus, we listen to these words according to John. Jesus says to us:

"In all truth, I tell you ..."

We must always respond to His words in all truth; with 'Amen', in affirmation of that revelation of Himself in truth. This truly is the beginning of all Christian prayer. It begins – **Amen**. So we read:-

> **John 16: 32, 33** *"Do you believe, at last? Listen, the time will come; indeed it has come already, When you are going to be scattered, each going his own way And leaving me alone. And yet I am not alone Because the Father is with me. I have told you all this so that you may find peace in me. In the world, you will have hardship but be courageous. I have conquered the world."*

The Apostle of Prayer

"It is not only when He is about to send some trial that Our Lord gives me warning and awakens my desires. For years I have felt a longing to have a brother who would be a priest, though I knew my desire could never be realised. I used to think that if my little brothers had not been taken to heaven, I should have had the happiness of seeing them at the Altar and I greatly regretted having been deprived of such joy. Yet God gave me joy far beyond this dream. I longed for one brother who would remember me each day at the Altar and God has united me in bonds of spiritual friendship with two of His apostles. I should like to tell you, dear Mother, how our Divine Master granted me this favour."

"In 1895, our holy mother, Saint Teresa, sent my first brother as a gift for my feast day. It was washing day and I was busy at my work when Mother Agnes of Jesus, then Mother Prioress, called me aside and read to me a letter from a young seminarian, in which he said he had been inspired by Saint Teresa to ask for a Sister who would devote herself specially to his salvation, together with that of the souls one day to be entrusted to him. He promised that following his ordination, he would always remember, in the Holy Sacrifice, the one who would become his sister in Christ. Thus it was that I was given this future missionary as my brother. I cannot express to you, my Mother, how happy I felt. Such unlooked for fulfilment of my desires awoke in my heart what can only be described as the joy of a child. It carried me back to those early years when pleasures were so keen that my heart seemed too small to contain them. Years had passed since I tasted such happiness. It was as if some forgotten chords had been stirred within me."

"Conscious of my new obligations, I tried my very best to discharge them and determined to redouble my fervour. Now and again I wrote to my brother. Beyond all doubt, it is by prayer and sacrifice we can best help our missionaries, yet sometimes when Our Lord is pleased to unite two souls for His glory, He permits them to exchange their thoughts and so to prompt one another to a greater love for God.

Such correspondence must, of course, depend entirely on the express desire of those in authority, otherwise it seems to me it may do more harm than good – if not to the missionary, then at least to the Carmelite whose life is so largely one of thought. For a correspondence carried on at her own request, even at distant intervals, instead of uniting her to God, would occupy her mind uselessly and perhaps lead her to believe that she was doing wonders, when in reality, under cover of zeal, she was simply procuring for herself a needless distraction.

Here I am, dear Mother, launched upon not a distraction but upon a dissertation, equally superfluous. I shall never correct myself of these lengthy digressions which you must find most wearisome. Forgive me, then, if I begin again at the next opportunity.

Last year, at the end of May, it was your turn to give me my second brother. When I proffered the objection that having given all my merits to one future Apostle, I feared they could not be given to another, you told me that obedience would double their value. In the depths of my heart I had felt certain of this, moreover, since the zeal of a Carmelite ought to embrace the whole world, I hope with God's help, to be of use to more than two missionaries. I pray for all, without forgetting our priests at home whose ministry is often as full of difficulties as that of the missionary preaching to the heathen. Like our

Mother, Saint Teresa, I must be a true daughter of the Church and pray for all the intentions of Christ's Vicar, the one great aim of my life".

> **Meditate.** *Saint Therese, may our merits be joined with yours and offered for our brother Priests, Apostles for our time. We unite ourselves with you, Saint Therese, in the little way of love and offer up all our merits for our Priesthood in Christ. May they be called to His service in serving us and may our prayers and little sacrifices be offered up for the fulfilment of their vocations at the Altar of God. This prayer unites us all in the joyful mission of saving souls; the great purpose of our Mother the Church.*
>
> *May our obedience in the collaborative ministry of the Church double the merits offered to the priestly ministry for the good of His Church and the greater Glory of God. With Saint Therese, we ask Mary, Mother of God, to offer this oblation through her Son, Jesus the Christ.*

"Just as I would have taken a special interest in the work of my own dear brothers, had they lived, without neglecting the general interest of the church, so now I unite myself in a special manner to the new brothers whom Jesus has given me. To each belongs all I possess, for God is too good, too generous, to divide my offerings. He is so rich that He gives without measure, all I ask, that I am not lost in lengthy enumerations. Since I have two brothers as well as my little Sisters, the novices, the day would be too short to ask in detail for the needs of each soul and I am afraid I might miss something important. Complicated methods are not for simple souls. As I am one of those, Our Lord Himself has inspired me with a very simple way of fulfilling my obligations."

> **Meditate.** *Saint Therese, in this little way of love, we ask Jesus to guide our lives, open our hearts and lift up our minds to heaven; that we, with His Church, make an unblemished sacrifice united to His mystical body, so that united in collaboration through the Holy Spirit, our little lives might be pleasing in support of all who minister in His name.*

One day, after Holy Communion, He gave me the understanding in truth, of these words of Solomon: "Draw me: we will run after you to the odour of your ointments." **(Song of Songs 1: 3–4)**

The text we should use is from the Jerusalem version and is, of course, the opening stanza in the voice of the Beloved and the first line of verse four, the First Poem:

> *Delicate is the fragrance of your perfume Your name is unction poured out and that is why girls love you. Draw me in your footsteps, let us run!*

This prologue to the Song of Songs, the *Canticle of Love*, sets the scene for the following epic love song. It is the keynote of passionate tenderness. This verse also uses the first and third person quite abruptly because, although 'the Lover' is absent, he is always in her heart. The Beloved companions know this and they associate themselves with this love and are known as the 'Daughters of Jerusalem'. The Song of Songs recalls to the reader's mind also **Psalm 45**, the Royal Marriage

Song. It is significant to understand that the Lover present in the Heart of the Beloved was experienced intensely by Saint Therese and that this explains her complete immersion into the Sacred Heart and, thus, to expressing the prayer of Jesus as her prayer.

O my Jesus, there is no need to say: in drawing me to you, draw also the souls that I love. The words 'draw me' are sufficient. When a soul has been captivated by the scent of your perfumes, she cannot run alone; it follows quite naturally that all whom she loves are drawn in her train.

As a torrent bears down to the depths of the seas, whatsoever it meets on the way, so my Jesus, does the soul that plunges into the boundless ocean of your love bring with it all its treasures. My treasures, as you know, are the souls it has pleased you to unite with mine and which you had confided to me. Therefore, I dare to borrow your own words, your prayer on the last night that knew you as a traveller on this earth. O my Beloved, I know not when my exile will end. For many nights yet I may sing of your mercies here below, but for me too, will come the last night of all, then I will be able to say: 'I have glorified you here on earth'.

> **Meditate. (John 17: 4–26)** *In the Prayer of Jesus according to John, the time for sacrifice draws near. In this prayer, Jesus offers Himself and intercedes for His Beloved disciples.*

> *I have glorified you on earth by finishing the work you gave me to do. So Father, glorify me with that glory I had with you before the world existed. I have revealed your name to those whom you took from the world to*

give me. They were yours and you gave them to me and they have kept your word. Now at last, they have recognised that all you have given me comes from you. For I have given them the teaching you gave to me and they have indeed accepted it and know for certain that I came from you and have believed that it was you who sent me. It is for them that I pray. I am not praying for the world but for those you have given me because they belong to you. All I have is yours and all you have is mine and in them I am glorified. I am no longer in the world and I am coming to you, Holy Father. Keep those you have given me true to your name so that they be one like us.

While I was with them, I kept those you had given me true to your name. I have watched over them and not one is lost, except the one who was destined to be lost and this was to fulfil the Scriptures. Now I am coming to you and say these things in the world to share my joy with them to the full. I passed your word on to them and the world hated them because they belong to the world no more than I belong to the world. I am not asking you to remove them from the world but to protect them from the evil one. They do not belong to the world any more than I belong to the world. Consecrate them in the truth, your word is truth. As you sent me into the world, I have sent them into the world and for their sakes I consecrate myself so that they too, may be consecrated in truth. I pray, not only for these, but also for those who through their teaching, will come to believe in me. May they all be one just as, Father, you are in me and I am in you so *that they may also be in us and the world may believe it was you who sent me. I have given them the glory you gave to me that they may be one as we are one.*

With me in them and you in me, may they be so perfected in unity that the world will recognise that it was you who sent me and that you have loved them as you have loved me. Father, I want those you have given me to be with me where I am so that they may always see my glory, which you have given me because you loved me before the foundation of the world. Father, Upright One, the world has not known you but I have known you and these have known that you have sent me. I have made your name known to them and will continue to make it known so that the love with which you loved me may be in them and so that I may be in them.

Jesus prays for His Church of believers in Him; they will be gathered in the barn and sheepfold by the witness of the Apostles and disciples. It is their unity, in the love of the Father of the Son, which will encourage faith in the mission of Jesus; this unity of Love is the true sign of Divine Love in Process, which is the Holy Trinity. The Church is a unity in Love, a perfection of community in Christ who is in the Father, that community is the Community of the Holy Spirit, sent by Jesus at Pentecost. The Father sent Jesus, Jesus sent the Holy Spirit, so that in Jesus the Christ, we return in perfect unity to the Creator. Thus the Doxology of the Mass, 'Through Him, with Him, in Him, in the unity of the Holy Spirit, all honour and glory is yours, almighty Father, for ever and ever.

Amen.

"Thus, dear Lord, I would repeat your words before losing myself in your loving embrace. Perhaps I am very daring; however, for a long time now you have not allowed me to be audacious before you.

You have said to me, as the father of the Prodigal Son, 'All I have is yours' **(Luke 15: 31)**; therefore, I use these Divine words to draw down favours from our heavenly Father upon all the souls under my care.

My God, you know that I have always desired to love you and you alone. I seek no other glory. Your love has gone before me from the days of my childhood. It has grown with me in my youth; it is now an ocean, the depth of which I cannot sound. Love attracts Love, and mine, in its flight like an arrow to you, desires to fill to the brim the ocean of love that draws it on. Sadly, my love is but a drop in that ocean. To love you as you love me, I must use your own love. This is the only way my desire of love can be satisfied. My Jesus, it seems to me that you have not seduced a soul with more love than you have poured into mine. That is why I can ask of you to love those you have given me, as you love me.

In heaven, if it is revealed that you loved them more than you love me, then I shall rejoice. I know that they deserve greater love than I do. However, here on earth I cannot conceive a love comparable to that which you give me, without any merit of mine.

That which I have written above, Mother, amazes me. I had no intention of saying such things. When I repeated this passage from the Gospel, 'the words which you gave to me I have given to them', I was not thinking of my brothers but only my little Sisters in the Noviciate for I do not consider myself capable of teaching missionaries. The words I wrote for them were taken from Our Lord's Prayer, 'I pray not that you should take them from this world … I pray also for those who through their word will come to believe in me!' How could I have overlooked the souls they win by their suffering and proclamation?"

> **Meditate.** *We meditate on the sublimity of God's love, of its intensity, its immensity, an ocean so vast it engulfs all. We rejoice in receiving this love as His Beloved and, in uniting ourselves in Him, a community of love and praise in thanksgiving is created. This is His Church, the power of His Sacred Heart lifts us up to pray through Him because Love attracts Love and speaks to us the Beloved of the promises of salvation. When we pray in Christ, we are drawn to Him and, drawing on His ocean of love, we invite others to come into the sanctuary of His loving presence. This is a witness with the Angels who sing God's praises in heaven, this is what the 'Sanctus' teaches us.*

The Saint continues,

"I have not yet fully explained my thoughts on the words of the Song of Songs, 'draw me, we will run'. Our Lord has said, 'No man can come to me unless drawn by the Father – who sent me' **(John 6: 44).** Further on He teaches us 'everyone who asks receives, everyone who searches finds, everyone who knocks will have the door opened'. Further He adds to this 'If you ask the Father anything in my name, He will give it to you'. Beyond any doubt then, long before the birth of Our Lord, the Holy Spirit dictated these prophetic words.

'Draw me, we will run.'

In asking to be drawn to Him, we seek an intimate union with the object of our love that has captured our hearts. If iron and fire were endowed with reason, the iron could say, 'Draw me'. This would prove its desire to be combined with the fire to the point of sharing its unity. Well, such is precisely my prayer. I ask Jesus to draw me into the fire of His love and to unite me so closely to Himself that He may live and act in me. I feel that the more the fire of love consumes my heart, the more frequently I shall exclaim, 'Draw me' and more also will the souls who come in contact with mine – 'Run swiftly in the sweet perfume of the Beloved.'

They will run, yes, we will run together, for souls that are on fire with love cannot remain inactive. They may certainly, like St Mary Magdalene, sit at the feet of Jesus listening to His soft and burning words, though appearing to give Him nothing, give more than Martha who was troubled about many things. It is not Martha's work that our Lord blames, for His own Blessed Mother humbly devoted herself to the same daily tasks, preparing meals for the Holy Family. What He blames is Martha's excessive concern for such things.

The power of prayer has been understood by all the Saints, especially those who have illuminated the world with Christ's teaching. Was it not in prayer that St Paul, St Augustine, St Thomas Aquinas, St John of the Cross, St Teresa and so many other friends of God acquired the wonderful knowledge which has enthralled the greatest minds?

'Give me a lever and a fulcrum on which to lean it and I will lift the world,' said Archimedes. What this scientist could not obtain, because his request had merely a material end, without reference to God, the Saints have obtained in all its fullness. The Almighty has given them as a fulcrum to lean on, Himself – Himself alone – and for a lever, the flame that lights the fire of love. Thus they have lifted up the world. Thus do the Saints who continue the fight here on earth raise up the world and continue to raise it until the end of time!

It remains now for me to tell you, dear Mother, what I understand by the sweet perfume of the Beloved. Since the Lord is in heaven, I can only know Him by the rays full of light and fragrance, which He has left behind. As soon as I open the Holy Gospels, I breathe the perfume exhaled by the life of Jesus and I know which way to run to Him. It is not to the highest place but to the lowest place that I hasten. Leaving the Pharisees to go forward, I repeat the humble prayer of the publican. Most of all I imitate the behaviour of the Magdalene, for her amazing, her loving audacity which delighted the heart of Jesus has cast its spell on mine. It is not merely because I have been preserved from mortal sin that I lift up my heart in trust and love, for I am sure that even if I had on my conscience every imaginable crime, my confidence would not be shaken. I would throw myself, with my broken heart in sorrow, into the arms of my Saviour. I remember His love for the Prodigal Son; I have heard His words to St Mary Magdalene, to the woman taken in adultery and to the Samarian woman. No, there is no one who could frighten me, for I know so well what to believe of His mercy and love.

In the Lives of the Fathers of the Desert, it is written how one of them converted a public sinner whose evil deeds were the scandal of the whole country. Touched by grace, the sinful woman followed the Saint into the desert to perform a rigorous penance. On the first night of the journey, before she reached the place of her retirement, the vehemence of her love and sorrow broke the ties that bound her to earth. The Holy man, at that moment, saw her soul borne by the angels to the bosom of God. This is a dramatic and fine illustration of my message, but the reality itself, is beyond the power of words to express."

> **Meditate.** *Prayer, in its power to unite us with Jesus Christ in the Holy Trinity, is the result of His love which draws us up to the Father's arms. We run to the Beloved to behold Him in the Blessed Sacrament and receive Him in Holy Communion – a communion so profound that it unites us to the Godhead itself. In this communion, this Sunday, we ask that we should become active in the fire of His love and run after Him that all the world will witness our rejoicing.*
>
> ***Alleluia!***

Chapter 4

Catechist and Teacher

C.C.C. 2011 From the Catechism of the Catholic Church. Note 63, Saint Therese, 'Act of Offering'. *The Charity of Christ is the source in us of all merits before God. Grace, by uniting us to Christ in active love, ensures the supernatural quality of our acts and consequently their merit before God and before men. (see below)*

C.C.C. 127 The fourfold Gospel has a unique and most exulted place in the Church. This is evident in the veneration given in the Liturgy. It is simply at the heart of all liturgy. Also, it is the inspiration and font of wisdom for all the Saints.

This is the message of Saint Caesarea the Younger to Saint Rachel and Saint Radegunde Sch. (Sources Chrétienne's) 345,480.

"There is no better doctrine, more precious and more splendid than the text of the Gospel. Read and retain, listen and remember, what our Lord and Master, Christ taught by His words and accomplished by His deeds. But above and beyond all, it is the Gospel that occupies my mind when I am at prayer. My poor soul has so many needs, yet this is the one thing which fulfils those needs. I am always finding fresh illumination there, hidden meanings which I had not grasped before." **Saint Therese of Lisieux.**

C.C.C. 826 Charity is the soul of the holiness to which all are called: It governs shapes and perfects all the ways and means of sanctification.

"If the Church is a body composed of different organs, it cannot lack the noblest of all organs. It must have a heart. A heart burning with love. I realised that this is love alone, the true motive force which enables all the other organs of the Church to act. If it ceased to function, the Apostles would forget to preach the Gospel, the martyrs would refuse to shed their blood. Love, in fact, is THE VOCATION, WHICH INCLUDES ALL OTHERS. IT IS A UNIVERSE OF ITS OWN, COMPRISING ALL TIME AND SPACE – IT IS ETERNAL." Saint Therese.

The intercession of the Saints, "Being more closely united to Jesus Christ, those who dwell in heaven act to bring the 'Whole Church' more firmly fixed in holiness. They do not cease to intercede with the Father for us, as they offer themselves and lives here on earth, through the one mediator between God and man, Jesus Christ. So that by their familial concern, they strengthen our resolve and weakness to move forward in Christ to our Salvation."

Saint Dominic, on his deathbed, spoke to his brothers, "Do not weep, for I shall be more useful to you after my death, for then I will help you more effectively than during my life."

Saint Therese, in her final conversations, teaches us and asks of God, "I want to spend my heaven in doing good on earth."

C.C.C. 1011 In death, God calls man to Himself. There, as Christians, we can experience a desire for death as St Paul tells us, "My desire is to depart and be with Christ." **(Philippians 1: 23.)** Christians can transform their own death into an act of obedience and love for the Father after the example of Christ.

St Ignatius of Antioch said, "My earthly desire has been crucified ... there is living water in me, water that murmurs and says within me, 'Come to the Father'."

St Teresa of Avila said, "I want to see God and in order to see Him, I must die."

Saint Therese said in her Little Way, "I am not dying, I am entering life."

In the section of the Catechism, under the heading 'Man's Vocation, Life in the Spirit', the Church teaches us: The Charity of Christ is the source in us of all our merits before God, by uniting us to Christ in active love, we are ensured of the supernatural quality of our acts and, consequently, their worthiness before God and to mankind. The Saints have always been at one in the understanding that their lives, in goodness, were pure grace.

So the Church teaches us with the words of Saint Therese: "After earth's exile, I hope to go with joy in the home of Our Father but I do not want to store up any merits in heaven. I want to work for your love alone. In the evening of this life, I shall appear before you with empty hands, for I do not ask you, Lord, to count my works. All our justice is blemished in your eyes. I yearn then to be clothed in your own justice and to receive from your love, the eternal possession of yourself."

C.C.C. 2559 The last section of the Catechism of the Catholic Church has the inspiring title: 'Prayer in the Christian Life.'

C.C.C. 2558 'Great is the mystery of the Faith!' The Church professes this mystery in the Apostle's Creed (Part I) and celebrates it in the sacramental liturgy (Part II), so that the life of the faithful may be conformed to Christ in the Holy Spirit to the Glory of God the Father (Part III). This mystery requires then, that the faithful believe in it, that they celebrate it and that they live from it in a vital and personal relationship with the living and true God. This relationship is prayer.

C.C.C. 2559 What is Prayer?

Saint Therese is the teacher the Church has given for the answer to that question.

"For me, prayer is a surge of the heart, it is a simple look turned toward heaven. It is a cry of recognition and of love, embracing both trial and joy."

Letters to the Brother Missionaries

(AD1895) Our Divine Lord asks for no sacrifice beyond our strength. At times, it is true, He makes us taste to the full, the bitterness of the chalice He puts to our lips. When He demands the sacrifice of all that is dearest on earth, it is impossible without a very special grace to call out, as He did during His agony in the garden, "My Father, let this chalice pass from me!" He hastened to add, "Nevertheless, not as I will but as thou wilt." **(Matthew. 26: 39.)** It is consoling beyond measure to recall Jesus, 'the Strong God'.
   (Isaiah. 9: 6):

> *For a son has been born for us, a son has been given to us and dominion has been laid on His shoulders and this is the name He has been given, 'Wonderful*

*Counsellor', 'Mighty God', 'Eternal Father', 'Prince
of Peace', to extend His dominion in boundless peace
over the throne of David and over His Kingdom, to
make it secure and sustain it in fair judgement and
integrity.*

He has felt all our weaknesses and shuddered at the sight
of the bitter chalice – that very chalice He had so ardently
desired. Your lot is indeed a beautiful one since Our Lord
has chosen it for you and has first touched with His own lips
the chalice which He holds out to you. A saint has said, "The
greatest honour God can bestow upon a soul is not to give it
great things but to ask of it great things." Jesus treats you as
a privileged child. It is His wish that you should begin your
mission at once and save souls through the cross. [This letter
is to a seminarian.] Was it not by suffering and death that He
ransomed the world? I know that you aspire to the happiness
of laying down your life for Him, but the martyrdom of the
heart is no less fruitful than the shedding of blood and this
martyrdom is already yours. Have I not then, good reason
to say that your lot is a beautiful one, the worthiness of the
Apostle of Christ.

(AD1896 II) Let us work together for the salvation of souls.
We have but the one day of this life to save them, so to give
Our Lord a proof of our love. Tomorrow will be eternity, then
Jesus will reward you a hundredfold for the sweet joys you
have given up for Him. He knows the extent of your sacrifice.
He knows that the sufferings of those you hold dear increase
your own suffering, but He has suffered this same martyrdom
for our salvation. He too, left His mother; He saw the sinless

virgin standing at the foot of the cross, her heart pierced through with a sword of sorrow. I hope He will console your own dear mother. I beg Him most earnestly to do so. Ah, that the Divine Master would permit those you are about to leave, for His love alone, one glimpse of the Glory awaiting you, as the vast retinue of souls escort you to heaven. They would realise themselves already recompensed for the great sacrifice that is at hand.

(24th February 1896 III) Please say this little prayer for me each day – it sums up all my desires.

Merciful Father, in the name of your Sweet Jesus of the Blessed Virgin, and all the Saints, I plead that you consume my sister with your spirit of love and grant her the grace to make you greatly loved.

If the Lord takes me soon to Himself, I ask you nonetheless, to continue this prayer, because my longing will be the same in heaven as it was on earth – to love Jesus and to Make Him loved.

I will not be idle in heaven, for it is my wish to continue to work for the Church and for the salvation of souls. I ask this grace from God and I am certain He will grant it. So, as I am leaving the battlefield, it is not with the selfish desire of taking my rest. It is a long time since suffering became my paradise on earth and I find it difficult to understand how I shall be acclimatised in a place where joy reigns supreme and alone. Jesus must radically change this soul of mine for otherwise it cannot endure perfect bliss.

All I desire is God's Holy will and if in Heaven I could no longer work for His Glory, I would prefer exile here to home.

(21st June 1897) You sing well of the mercies of God. They shine forth in you with great splendour. Your love of St Augustine and St Mary Magdalene, those souls who had many sins forgiven because they loved so much. I love them too. I love their penitent sorrow and affectionate daring. When I see Mary Magdalene come out among Simon's guests to wash, with her tears, the Master's feet as she touches them for the first time. I feel her heartbeat has plumbed the depths of His love and mercy, the very heart of Jesus. I feel too, that not only was He willing to forgive, but generously bestowed the divine favours of intimate friendship that raised her up to the supreme heights of prayer.

My brother, as I too have been given the awareness of the love of the heart of Jesus, I proclaim that all fear has left my heart. As I remember my faults, I am humbled and I am assisted in the knowledge that I can never rely upon my own strength, for my strength is mere weakness. More than this, my humbled heart speaks of mercy and love. When a soul with childlike trust throws her faults into love's all-consuming fire, they cannot escape being utterly consumed.

I am aware that many saints passed their lives in the practice of stupendous penance for the sake of expiating their sins. How should we look upon this? 'In my Father's house, there are many rooms.' These are the words of Jesus and I follow that path which He marks out for me. I endeavour not to be concerned with myself and to abandon myself to Him with all the work He gives me to accomplish for the sanctification of my soul.

The Little Way – (1897 VI) On this earth, where everything changes, one thing alone never changes; our Heavenly King's treatment of His friends. From the day He raised the standard of the Cross, in its shadow we all must fight and win. "The life of every missionary abounds in crosses," said Theophane Venard [martyred at the age of 32, he was beatified in 1909], and again he said, "True happiness consists in suffering, in order to live we must die."

Rejoice, dear brother, that the first efforts of your Apostolate are stamped with the seal of the Cross. Jesus builds His Kingdom more by persecution and suffering than by eloquent discourses.

You are, so you tell me, a little child who cannot preach. Neither could Father Mazel who was ordained with you and yet he has already won the palm. How God's acts are so much in excess of our own. When I learnt that this young missionary had died before he set foot upon the battlefield, I was drawn by the love of God to invoke him in prayer. I saw him, in the mind's eye, amidst the glorious martyrs' choir. Men will doubt he merits the title of martyr, but in the sight of God, this inglorious death is as precious as the sacrifice of him who lays down his life for faith.

Although we must be perfect before appearing in the sight of the All Holy God, I know that He is infinitely just and this justice which terrifies so many souls is a source of all my confidence and joy. Justice is not only stern severity to the guilty; it weighs also the good intention and gives to virtue its great reward. I hope as much from the Justice of God as from His mercy. It is because He is the Just One that He revealed to us:

Psalms. 103: 8–13 & 14 *Yahweh is all tenderness and pity, slow to anger and rich in faithful love. As tenderly as a Father treats his children so Yahweh treats those who fear Him. He knows of what we are made, He remembers that we are dust.*

O my brother, when we have heard these beautiful and inspiring words of the Royal Prophet, how can we doubt God's power to open the gates of His kingdom to the children who have loved Him unto perfect sacrifice? Who have not only left home and country to make Him known and loved, but to lay down their lives for Him? Jesus said, "Truly there is no greater love than this." Nor can we outdo Him in generosity. How could He need to cleanse souls in the flames of Purgatory, those consumed with the fire of Divine Love? I have used many words to express my reflections but without success. I wish to say that, in my opinion, all missionaries are martyrs by will and desire and that none should need to pass through the purifying flames.

These then are my thoughts upon the Justice of God, my own way is all confidence and love and I do not understand those souls who are afraid of so affectionate a friend. Sometimes, as I read books in which perfection is presented as the goal obstructed by a thousand obstacles, my little head aches with fatigue. I close those learned tomes which tire my brain and dry up my heart and I turn to Sacred Scripture. Then all becomes clear, a single word reveals vast horizons, perfection appears easy. I realise that it is enough to acknowledge one's nothingness and surrender oneself to His arms like an affectionate child. Leaving to great and high minds the beautiful books which I cannot understand, still less put into practice, I rejoice in my littleness; 'only little children and those who are like them shall be admitted to the Heavenly Banquet'. It is fortunate that 'There are many rooms in my Father's house'; if there were to exist those incomprehensible mansions with their baffling approaches, I could certainly never enter there …

(July 1897) Your soul is too great to cling to the consolations of earth. Even now its abode should be in heaven, for it is written, 'Where your treasure is, there will your heart be also' **(Luke 12: 34).** He is in Paradise and it is there that your heart should dwell. Our sweet Saviour has long since forgotten your infidelities. He sees only your longing after perfection. Is not Jesus your only treasure? The sight of your longing after perfection rejoices His heart.

Stay no longer at His feet, I beseech you. Follow instead your first impulse and throw yourself into His arms. Your place is there, I see clearly, more clearly than in your former letters, that every other road to heaven is barred to you save the way your little sister treads. I agree with you that the heart of Jesus is more grieved by the thousand little imperfections of His friends than by the faults, however grave, of His enemies. Yet it seems to me, dear brother, it is only when those who are His own are habitually guilty of wont of thought and who neglect to seek His pardon, that he says, "These wounds in my hands I have received from those of my house, who love me." His heart is thrilled with joy when He comes to those who love truly and who, following each transgression, come and fling themselves into His arms, imploring forgiveness. He says to His angels what the Prodigal's Father said to his servants, "Put a ring on his finger and let us rejoice." My brother, how little known is the merciful love of the Heart of Jesus. It is true that to enjoy such treasure we must humble ourselves, confess our poverty; this is where many souls draw back.

(1897) What attracts me to our heavenly home is our Master's call, the hope at last of loving Him to the fulfilment of all my desires; the thought that I shall be able to win for Him, the love of the multitude of souls who will Bless Him through all eternity. I have never asked God that I might die young – it would have seemed a cowardly prayer – but from childhood, He has inspired me with a strong conviction that my life on earth will be short.

I feel I must tread His same road to heaven, the road of suffering and love. When I reach port, I will teach you how to sail the world's tempestuous seas, with the self-abandonment of a child intensely aware of its Father's love and His vigilance in every hour of danger.

I yearn to make you aware of the expectant love of the heart of Jesus. Your letter has made my heart thrill sweetly. I learnt how close is your sister soul to mine, since God calls it to rise to Himself by the updraught of love, far from the staircase of fear. I am not surprised that you find it difficult to be familiar with Jesus. This is not possible in a day so I shall be able to assist you far more on this beautiful pathway when I lay aside my mortal frame. A little while longer and you will exclaim with St Augustine, "Love it is that draweth me."

(26th July 1897) When you read these few lines, I will perhaps be no more. I do not know the future, yet it is with confidence that I say my Spouse is at the door. It would need a miracle to keep me here in exile and I do not think that Jesus will work one since He does nothing that is useless. Brother, I am so happy to die. Yes happy, not because I shall be free of suffering – on the contrary, suffering bound up with love is the one thing worthy of desire in this vale of tears. I shall be happy to die because I will be far more able to help the souls I hold most dear. Jesus has always treated me as a spoilt child. It is true that His cross has been with me since the cradle but with that cross, He has given me passionate Love.

(14th August 1897) I am about to go before God. I understand now more than ever that one thing only is needful, to work for Him alone and not for oneself or for creatures. Jesus wants to own your heart completely. Before this can be, you will have much to suffer but what joy when the hour comes and it is time to go home. I shall not die – I do but enter into life.

> **Meditate.** *O God, so visible and yet forgotten. O God, so simple in beauty that we pass by. O God, the heart of Jesus burns with love yet we cling to the wastelands here on earth. Jesus, we come to you with open hearts full of unbounded love. We come in our poverty asking you for the treasure of the Kingdom of heaven.*
>
> *Our poverty is the vessel of your riches. We empty ourselves to be filled with your love. We long to be with Our Father in heaven. We rejoice in the Holy Spirit in His Church. Lord, we are dressed in our wedding garments, the garments given to us at Baptism. We throw ourselves into your loving embrace. Little ones of Saint Therese, we are coming home. There is great joy in our little hearts because we know of your greatness. We long for our love to flower in your hands in Paradise. All we have has been given by you.*

Jesus, your love overwhelms. Your call is sweet and draws us on. Like children, we run in laughter to Our Father, asking His protection, His forgiveness at our thousand little faults. Father, Son and Holy Spirit, we plunge into that fire of love. We know how your mercy, your strength, your love draw us on to perfection. Perfect us in the perfection of your love that we are made worthy of the embrace, the embrace of compassion and love.

With the choirs of Heaven singing your praises for the eternal Salvation of all souls.

BWF

Amen.

Chapter 5

The Little Way

D EAR MOTHER,

You have expressed a desire that I should finish singing the mercies of the Lord.

'**The mercies of the Lord, I will sing forever**', this was the motto of Saint Teresa of Avila and though I make no protest, I am amused as I take up my pen once more. What I write, you already know as well as I do, yet I obey. I do not ask what use this manuscript could be and should you burn it, in my presence unread, I would not be distressed in any way.

> **Psalm 89** *This psalm most dear to Saint Teresa and Saint Therese closes the third book of the Psalter; therefore, it concludes in a Doxology:*
> **Blessed be Yahweh for ever.**
> **Amen, Amen.**

This psalm opens with a prologue, verses one and two, which is a summary of the foundation of the collaborative ministry of the **Little Way**. We may sing.

I shall sing the faithful love of Yahweh for ever. From age to age my lips shall declare your constancy for you have said in my heart, love is built to last forever. You have fixed your constancy firm in the Heavens.

The next two verses, three and four, are a hymn to the Creator:

I have made a covenant with my Chosen One, sworn an oath to my servant David.
I have made your dynasty firm forever, built your throne, stable age after age.

This is the Davidic covenant, the typology for which, in Christ, becomes the new and everlasting Covenant through the Incarnation. This is followed in verses five to eighteen with the infallible oracle revealed in scripture as to the angels who intercede for us in Heaven.

The heavens praise your wonders, Yahweh, your constancy in the gathering of your faithful. Who in the skies, can compare with Yahweh? Who among the sons of God can rival him? God, awesome in the assembly of the Holy Ones, Held in awe among all who surround Him. Yahweh, God, who is like you? Mighty God, your constancy is all around you. You control the pride of the ocean.

When its waves ride high, you calm them. You split Rahab in two like a corpse. You scatter your enemies with a mighty arm. Yours are the heavens, yours the earth. The world and all it holds, you founded them. You created the North and the South. Tabor and Herman hail your name with joy.

Yours is a strong arm, Mighty your hand, your right hand raised high saving justice and fair judgement, The foundations of your throne. Faithful love and constancy march before you.

How Blessed the nation that was born to acclaim you; they will live, Yahweh, in the light of your presence. In your name they rejoice all day long; by your saving justice they are raised up.

You are the flower of their strength; by your grace our strength is triumphant for to Yahweh belongs our shield to the Holy One of Israel, our King.

In this next section we hear of the constancy of Yahweh, His covenant with David which will last forever. This throne of David is the 'Rock of His Salvation'. He is the firstborn – the King of Kings.

Once you spoke in a vision. To your faithful, you said, "I have given strength to the warrior, I have raised up a man chosen from my people.

I have found David, my servant and Anointed him with my holy oil. My hand will always be with him, my arm will make him strong.

No enemy will be able to outwit him, No wicked man overcome him. I shall crush his enemies before him, strike his opponents dead.

My constancy and faithful love will be with him. In my name his strength will be triumphant. I shall establish his power over the sea, his dominion over the rivers.

He will cry to me, 'You are my Father, my God, the Rock of my Salvation.' So I shall make him my first born, the highest of earthly Kings.

I shall maintain my faithful love for him always, my covenant with him will stay firm. I have established his dynasty for ever, his throne to be as lasting as the heavens. Should his descendants desert my law and not keep my rule. Should they violate my statutes and not keep my commandments, then I shall punish their offences with the rod, their guilt with the whip. But I shall never withdraw my faithful love. I shall not belie my own constancy.

I shall not violate my covenant. I shall not withdraw the word once spoken. I have sworn my holiness once for all, never will I break faith with David.

His dynasty will endure forever, his throne like the sun before me, as the moon is established forever, a faithful witness in the skies."

Verses thirty-eight to forty-five tell of further sufferings and humiliation brought down upon the Kingdom by His people – His own have rejected Him.

Yet you yourselves have spurned and rejected and vented your spleen upon the anointed. You have repudiated your covenant with your servant, dishonoured his crown in the dust. You have pierced all his defences and laid his strongholds in ruin. Everyone passing by plunders him, he has become the butt of his neighbours. You have raised the right hand of his opponents, have made all his enemies happy. You have broken his sword on a rock and failed him in battle. You have stripped him of his sceptre and toppled his throne to the ground. You have aged him before his time, shrouding him in shame.

This history of suffering and humiliation of Israel is ended by a great unfolding prayer. This prayer is a cry to faithfulness and love as the saving action of our God.

How long, Yahweh, will you remain hidden? Forever? Is your anger to go on smouldering like an underground fire? Remember me, how long have I left? For what futile end did you create the children of Adam? Who can live and never see death? Who can save himself from the grasp of Sheol?

Lord, what of your pledges of faithful love? You made an oath to David from your constancy, do not forget the insults to your servants. I am heart-stricken by the taunts of the nations which your enemies have voiced, Yahweh. They have mired the footsteps of your anointed.

Blessed be Yahweh for ever.
Amen, Amen!

The Saint continues: "It is held by many in the community that you have indulged me ever since I entered Carmel. It is written however, that 'man sees and understands through appearances, but the Lord sees into our hearts'. I thank you, Mother, for not having spared me. Jesus knew that His flower was too frail to take root without the life-giving waters of humbleness. It is to you then she owes that priceless blessing.

For some months, the Divine Master has changed His method of cultivation. Noting that His flower is well watered, He encourages her in growth with the warm rays of a brilliant sun. He smiles on her now and your smile, dear Mother, is the mirror of His. The bright sunlight does not wither the petals but fosters their growth in a wonderful way. Deep in her heart she treasures those precious drops of moisture; the humiliations of past days, they recall for her how frail she is. Were all creatures to draw near and pour out flattery, this would give no satisfaction because it is with joy that I realise that in the sight of God, she is poor and worthless and nothing more. When I say that I am indifferent of praise, I do not mean that I reject the love and confidence that you show for me – these things touch my heart. However, I do not fear praise any more because I can listen to it unmoved. I attribute to God all that is good in me. If it pleases Him that I appear better than I am, that is no concern of mine, He acts as He wills!"

> **Meditate.** *Humility is like His Crown of thorns, it makes certain that our adornments, though much admired, are acknowledged as His unmerited gifts to us. He has crowned His people with joy in the expression of His love for us. This tent of clay is most fragile for it holds the works of His faithful love for us. His love has forged our hearts with spiritual life so that we can soar with the Angels' host and walk humbly with our God. For in the Spirit, with the Holy Spirit, we grow close to Him, Our Saviour and friend. We grow into His perfection on the spiralled path of humility. Step by step we are led into living in His presence. We bend*

in prayer and remain upright in our hearts. For in perfection we become children of the light, the flowers of the meadows in heaven. In Paradise, we shall walk and talk with Him and see Him face to face. For in perfection, we are marked out for Him and as children all we have to delight Him are the flower petals of our hearts.

"My God", the Saint prays, "how wonderfully diverse are the ways you lead souls to perfection. We read of saints who left nothing behind them at their death, nothing by which they will be remembered, not a single line. In contrast others, like Saint Teresa, have adorned the Church with their sublime teaching. Never afraid to reveal the secrets of the Divine King that He be better known and loved. Which of these ways is more pleasing to God? To me it seems that each way is welcomed by Him. All those beloved by God have followed the inspiration of the Holy Spirit who commanded the prophet to write, 'Tell the just man that all is well.' Yes, all is well when we seek out the Master's will. So I, poor little flower, obey Jesus when I set out to please you, who represent Him here on earth.

You know, Mother, that I have always desired to be a Saint. In comparison with them, however, I have always felt that I am as far from them as a grain of sand trodden underfoot by the passer-by is from the mountain whose summit is lost in the clouds. Indeed, I feel discouraged by such reflections and I conclude that God would not foster a desire which cannot be fulfilled. So, then I know in spite of my smallness, I should aim to become a Saint.

It is impossible, I said, for me to become great so I must be reconciled to myself and my many imperfections. Yet I will still seek out a means of reaching heaven by a 'little way', very short, very straight and entirely new. We live in a time of inventions; there are now lifts which save us from climbing stairs. I will try to find a lift by which I may be raised to God, for I am too small to climb the steep stairway to perfection.

I sought to find in Holy Scripture, some promptings of what this elevator might be and I came across these words uttered by Wisdom herself, 'Whosoever is a little one, let him come unto me.' I therefore drew near to God assured that I had found what I sought. I sought to know what He would do for this 'little one'! I continued my search and this is the treasure I found:

"You will be carried at the breast and set upon the knee, as one who the Mother caresses, so will I comfort you". (**Isaiah. 66: 12–13**)

Never have I been consoled by such tender words, words so sweet, O Jesus. Your arms then, are the lift which must raise me to heaven. To reach heaven I do not need to become great. On the contrary I must remain little. I must become smaller than I am. My God, you have over-reached my desire and I will sing of your mercies! Thou has taught me Lord, from my youth, until now I have proclaimed your wonders and shall do so into old age with grey hair."

Psalm 71 A prayer in old age, of the House of Israel and the Child Isaac.

> *In you, Yahweh, I take refuge, I shall never be put to shame. In your saving justice, rescue me and deliver me. Listen to me and save me. Be a shelter of rock for me, always accessible. You have chosen to save me for*

you are my rock, my fortress. My God, rescue me from the grasp of the wicked, from the grip of the rogue and the ruthless. For you are my hope, Lord, my trust, Yahweh, since boyhood. On you I have relied since birth, since my mother's womb you have been my portion, the constant theme of my praises.

The Psalmist compares Israel to the birth of Isaac and the deeds of Abraham. Israel is a person born of God. The people are compared to the Love of the Father for His Son. This incarnational poetic inspiration is fulfilled in Jesus the Christ, and Saint Therese understands the Psalmist in his address to God as a teacher addressing a child.

Many were bewildered at my suffering but you are my sure refuge. My mouth is full of your praises, filled with your splendour all day long. Do not reject me in my old age nor desert me when my strength is failing for my enemies are discussing my weakness; those who have designs on my life are plotting together. Hound him down for God has deserted him. Seize him, there is no one to rescue him.' God, do not stand aloof, God, come quickly to my help.

The plea to be rescued from the evil clutches of death is a great theme of the Psalter. It is to God's mercy that the tradition of Israel returns. The plea is to God's love for His little one, as well understood by the Saint.

Shame and ruin on all those who slander me. May those intent on harming me be adorned with insult and infamy. As for me, my hope will never fade. I will praise you more and more. My lips shall proclaim your saving justice, your saving power all day long.

Therese tells us she hopes as much in God's Justice as in His mercy. His Saving Justice is the seat of His mercy because the Justice of God welcomes and brings about our salvation. This is His will, acted out in the Incarnation.

I shall come in the power of Yahweh to tell of your justice, yours alone. God you have taught me from childhood and I am still proclaiming your marvels.

Therese teaches us that we shall be lifted up to heaven by the power of His arm, thus was she borne up, as the Psalmist says, 'in the power of Yahweh'. This is the little way, the child of Jesus lifted up to everlasting Love.

Now that I am old and grey-haired, God, do not desert me. For I have proclaimed the strength and gentleness of your arms to the generations yet to come, proclaimed your power and justice to the skies. You have done great things, God, who is like you? You have shown me much misery and hardship But you will give me life again, you will raise me up from the depths of the earth, prolong my old age and comfort me. For my part I will thank you on the lyre for your constancy, my God. I will play the harp in your honour, Holy One of Israel. My lips sing for joy as I play to you because you have redeemed me and all day long my tongue meditates on your Saving Justice. Shame and disgrace on all who intend harm.

The Saint continues: When will this old age come to me? Surely it is as well to come now as later. In the eyes of the Lord, two thousand are no more than twenty years, than a single day. Do not think, Mother, that your child is anxious to leave you, or that she believes that it is a greater grace to die in the morning rather than in the evening of life. What she longs for always and values above all things is to please her Lord. Now that He seems to come near and draws her to His heavenly home, her heart is full of gladness. She knows so well that to do good here on earth, God has no need of anyone and even less of her than others.

Meanwhile, dear Mother, I know your will; I am to carry out at your side, a work [as novice mistress] which is both sweet and easy and which I shall complete from heaven.

You have said to me as Our Lord said to Saint Peter, "Feed my lambs." I am amazed! I feel so little that I have asked you most earnestly to feed your lambs yourself and to keep me among them. In some part you have done as I asked, calling me 'companion' rather than 'mistress', yet you have bidden me to lead them through green pastures, to point out to them where the meadow grass is sweetest and best, and to warn them against the brilliant but poisonous flowers which they must never touch except to crush them underfoot.

How is it that my youth and inexperience have not frightened you? Are you not afraid that I shall let your lambs stray? In acting thus, you must have recalled that Our Lord is often pleased to give His wisdom to little ones.

On this earth, it is rare to find souls who do not measure God's Omnipotence by their own small-minded limitations. The world is ever ready to admit exceptions; to God alone that liberty is denied!

I know it has long been the custom to measure experience by age – in his youth, the Holy King David sang to the Lord

(Psalms ll9 & 141) 'I am very young and despised,' but in the same Psalm he goes on to say, 'I have an understanding greater than the ancients because I have sought your commandments.'

'Your word is a lamp to my feet and a light to my path. I have sworn to keep the judgement of your justice.'

You assured me one day in all prudence that the Divine Master was enlightening me and giving me the experience of years. I am now too little to be guilty of vanity, too little to try and prove my humility with high learning. I prefer then to witness in all sincerity that, 'He that is mighty has done great things for me' **(Luke 1: 49).** The greatest of all His gifts is that He has shown me my littleness and how then, of my own power, that I am incapable of doing anything good.

> **Meditate.** *In Creation God created good and, by the power of His love in us, we can freely act to be good and become, in Christ, perfect as He wills. We are touched by Divinity in the Incarnation and behold we know ourselves as children of God. In our poverty we come to God as we really are, as He made us for Himself. For in Him, the plenitude of richness knows no bounds. In the purity of perfection it is a gift that knows no end. Lord, make us wise like the little ones who listen to your word and follow obediently your call. Saint Therese, guide us to Him.*
>
> *Amen.*

Chapter 6

The Night of the Soul

Saint Therese tells us in addressing Mother Gonzaga of her night of the soul, her time of desolation. As we read and hear the Saint, our sister, it occurred to me that these descriptions of the 'Night of the Soul' are misunderstood often, as the described reality of 'a loss of faith'. However, this is apparently not so; what is lost is the known reality of divine things. We are reminded when we listen to the Saint, our little sister, that through her faith she was drawn to the reality of His presence. The 'odour of His sanctity drew her to Him'. Her matrix of the senses beheld Him, her spouse, in that web of reality, which is human understanding of existent things here on earth. This is that grasp of perfection in knowing God through faith; it is the exulted state of our loving brothers and sisters, saints in His Church. They have reached a summit like Calvary and have a vision in reality of things divine. Their faith has led them on that difficult journey to the Cloak of Wisdom. It is an exulted condition of our humanness and brings with it great happiness and joy. This is not the summit of our consummation in Christ as described by Saint Therese. This total immersion into the perfection of Divine Love requires the passage of a soul into nothingness in contrast to the Glory of His creation. It is the 'Beginning', the state of primeval emptiness awaiting the plenitude of perfection and this passage is sustained by the Saint's faith in Jesus the Christ alone. This is the way for all creation to return in salvation to Our Heavenly Father. All will be gathered up in Christ through our faith and given back to Our Heavenly Father.

We cannot lose our faith, we can deny it, we can ignore it, we can protest against it, but as His gift, it remains a treasure intact in our hearts.

However, to lose the compensations of trust and joyous hope in the knowledge of His presence is indeed to experience a terrible desolation of fog-laden darkness, the trial visited upon our little sister, Doctor of the Church.

So she writes: My soul has known trials of many kinds and I have suffered much down here. In my childhood I did so with sadness, now I find sweetness in all things, even the most bitter.

You know me intimately, dear Mother, and you may smile as you read these words, for has ever a soul appeared less tried than mine? However, if the martyrdom I have passed through for the past twelve months were visible, it would cause great surprise. Since it is your desire that I should describe it, I will attempt to do so but my words are inadequate and I shall fail to make manifest the reality of this trial. Last year during Lent, I felt stronger than ever and in spite of the fast observed in all its sweet rigour, I was perfectly well until the time of Holy Week. In the early hours of Good Friday – the memory is bliss – Jesus gave me the hope of soon joining Him in His most beautiful heaven.

Permission was not given for me to watch at the Altar of

Repose throughout Thursday night, so I returned to my cell at midnight. As I laid my head upon the pillow, I felt a stream of hot moisture rise up into my mouth. Thinking I was about to die, my heart was enraptured and almost broke with joy. I had put out the lamp so I constrained my curiosity till morning and went peacefully to sleep.

Rising at five o'clock, I recalled instantly that I had some good news to learn and going to the window, as I had expected, my handkerchief was saturated with blood. What hope filled my heart! I was convinced that on the anniversary of His death, my beloved had let me hear His first call. It was like a sweet distant murmur, heralding His joyful approach.

I attended Prime and Chapter with great fervour and went swiftly to kneel at your feet and confide my happiness to you. I felt no fatigue and not the slightest pain, so I had no difficulty in getting permission to finish Lent as I had begun. On this Good Friday, I shared in all the austerities of Carmel without any relaxation. Never had they been so sweet, the hope of soon entering heaven transported me with joy. When I returned to our cell in the evening of that happy day, I was full of joy and as I went quietly to sleep, Jesus gave me that same sign as on the previous night of my imminent entry into eternal life. My faith at this time was so clear and alive that the memory of heaven was my greatest delight. I could not believe it possible that there were wicked men without faith. I was sure that those who deny the existence of another world deny their own convictions.

During Easter, the time so full of light, Our Lord made me understand that there are in reality, souls without faith and hope who through the neglect of grace have lost those precious gifts, the only source of pure and lasting joy. He then allowed my own soul to be plunged into deepest gloom. The knowledge of heaven, so sweet from my earliest years, became for me an experience of torture and loss. This trial did not last for days or weeks, months now have passed in my agony and I await relief. I long to explain my feelings but it is beyond my power. One must have passed through this turmoil to know how black it is. I will try to illustrate my condition. It is as if I had been born in a land of thick impenetrable fog and that I had never looked upon nature in her smiling moods, that I had never known one single ray of sunshine. It is as if from my earliest childhood, I had heard of these things and knew of this country, that it was a real place, a place I aspired to and that this was not a fabulous tale invented by the inhabitants of this land of dark mist. It was an unquestionable truth, for the King of that sunlit country had come to dwell for thirty-three years in this land of darkness, though sorrowfully. 'The darkness did not comprehend that He was the light of the world.' (**John 1: 5**)

Let us recall this passage of John, so loved by our little sister.

> *In the beginning was the Word. The Word was with God And the Word was God. He was with God in the Beginning. Through Him all things come into being, Not one thing came into being except through Him. What has come into being is life in Him, Life that was the light of man. A light shines in the darkness And darkness cannot overpower it.*

> **Meditate.** *The first act of Creation is that God divided light from darkness that we in freedom and in faith,*

should come into the light of life in love. He is the light
and illuminates our faith that we can know the light
through God's creation here on earth. Our little sister
lights up our lives with the perfumed petals of her
presence with Jesus in heaven and in His Church, His
mystical body here on earth. Saint Therese, guide us
from our darkness into the light through your spouse,
Jesus the Christ.
   Amen.

Saint Therese proclaims, Dear Jesus, I your child believe firmly that you are the Divine Light. I ask pardon for my unbelieving brethren and I am willing to eat the bread of sorrow (the Passover bread, unleavened, the bread of sorrow!) as long as you will that I should. This is our Lenten suffering until He rises and we join Him reconciled in His death.

For the love of you, Jesus, she will sit at the table of bitterness where these poor sinners take their food and she will not rise from her place until you make the sign. In her own name and in the name of her guilty brethren she prays:

O God, be merciful to us sinners **(Luke 18: 13)**, send us away from this table of anguish justified in you!

May all those on whom faith does not shine at last see the Light. My God, if the table which they profane needs to be purified by one who loves you, I am willing to remain there alone to eat the bread of massoth until the day when it shall please you to draw me into your Kingdom of Light. I ask no favour other than I should never offend you.

I have already told you, Mother that from childhood I had the conviction that I would one day be set free from this land of darkness. I believed it not only from what I had heard but also because, from the deepest longings of my heart, I was assured that there was a place reserved for me in a most beautiful country, a dwelling place for all eternity. It is comparable to the confidence of Christopher Columbus in anticipating the discovery of the New World. Suddenly, imperceptibly, the fog of incomprehension seeps into my very soul. It so blinds me that I no longer have the vision of the loveliness of my promised home, it has faded away.

When my heart, weary of the pall of this all-enveloping darkness, tries to find rest and strength in the thought of everlasting life to come, my anguish grows greater. The darkness borrows the voice of the unbeliever and mocks me, "You dream of a land of light and fragrance! You dream that the Creator of these wonders will be yours forever. You dream that one day you will enjoy escape from these mists in which you languish! Hope on, hope ever. Look forward to death, I will give you not what you hope for but, instead, a night still darker, a night of nothingness."

This description of my suffering, dear Mother is as far removed from reality as a painter's rough sketch of the model he copies. To write anymore precisely might be to blaspheme! Even now I may have said too much! May God forgive me. He knows how I try to live by faith even though it brings me no consolation. I have made more acts of faith during this past year than in all the rest of my life put together. Whenever the enemy provokes me to combat, I try to behave like a gallant soldier.

I am aware that this duel is an act of cowardice, so I turn my back on this foe without acknowledging his presence. Then I hasten to my Saviour to tell Him that I am ready to die, to shed my blood as witness to my belief in heaven. I tell Him that if, for this, He will open it for eternity to poor unbelievers, I am content to sacrifice during my life all joy in the vision of the heavenly home that awaits me.

So despite this trial which deprives me of all sense of enjoyment, I can still pray, 'Thou hast given me, O Lord, a delight in all your works'. **(Psalms. 92: 4)**

> *You have brought me joy, Yahweh, by your deeds. At the work of your hands I cry out, 'How great are your works, Yahweh, immensely deep your thoughts!' Dull people cannot realise this, fools do not grasp it.*

For is there a source of greater joy than to suffer for your Love, O my God? The more intense and hidden the suffering, the more is its value to you. In the impossible event that you should not be aware of my suffering, I would be happy to bear with it, in the sure hope that my tears may prevent or atone for just one sin against faith. You may wonder, am I exaggerating the bleakness of the night of my soul? If you were to judge by the poems I have composed this year, it would appear that I have been flooded with consolations, that I am a child for whom the veil of faith has been drawn aside. This night is not a veil; it is a wall that reaches to the very heavens, blotting out the starlit sky.

When I sing most fervently in my verse of the happiness of heaven, I feel no joy, I sing of only what I wish to believe. Sometimes in this struggle with darkness, I confess that a faint ray of sunshine glimmers in the dark night and brings me a moment of relief, but as it fades, the memory of it, instead of consoling me, makes the ensuing blackness more dense and implacable.

Yet I know that I have never experienced with greater intensity, the sweetness and mercy of the Lord. He did not give me this heavy cross when it would, I believe, have discouraged me but gave it to me when I could bear its weight. Now it does no more than deprive me of all natural satisfaction in my longing for heaven. It seems to me, Mother, that nothing prevents me from going there. I no longer have any great ambitions beyond that of living until I die of love!

I am free and I fear nothing not even that which I dreaded more than any other thing, a long illness that would make me a burden on the community. Should it please God, I am content that my sufferings of body and soul be prolonged for many years. I do not draw back from a long life or refuse the struggle. 'The Lord is the rock on whom I make my stand, who teaches my hands for war and my fingers for battle. My faithful love, my bastion, my citadel, my Saviour, I shelter behind Him, my shield.' **(Psalms. 144: 1–2)**

I have never asked God to let me die young but I have always thought that this favour will be granted me.

> **Meditate.** *Through a glass darkly we behold the wonders of God's creation. In this clouded vision, His beauty and the perfection of His call, we come to a faded vista of the glories of heaven. Through our little sister we ask that, in prayer, we be lifted up to behold the divine light of His love. In your sacrifice, Jesus, you have redeemed us; may we remain ever worthy of such love. Come to us so that with your saints, we may ever praise and give you thanks. We ask God to guide us and keep us ever in His company, the company of the only begotten Son, Our Saviour, Jesus the Christ.*

> *Saint Therese, walk with us in the meadow of His prayer. Keep us close in your company that we shall sing the Psalms with you in Heaven.*

Very often He is satisfied with our desire to labour for His glory. You know, Mother, how intense my desire. You are aware too, in my own dearly beloved sisters, Jesus has given me more than one bitter chalice. The Holy King David was in harmony with God when he sang 'Behold, how delightful it is for brethren to sit down as a community together' **(Psalms. 153: 1**). Perfect union can only exist on earth in the midst of sacrifice. It was not to live with my sisters that I came to this dear Carmel. I foresaw clearly that in restraining natural affection, there would be great scope for suffering.

How can we understand the saying, 'it is more perfect to separate ourselves from those who are bound to us by ties of blood'? Are brothers to be blamed who fight side by side on the same battlefield or who together win the martyr's palm? It is true that they encourage one another but it is also the case that each individual martyrdom inflicts a martyrdom on all. It is like this in the religious life which theologians call a martyrdom. A heart given totally to God loses nothing of its natural affection; on the contrary that affection grows stronger, purer and more spiritual. It is with this love, Mother, that I love you and my sisters. I am ecstatic to fight beside you for the glory of the King of Heaven. Yet I am ready to go to another battlefield should our Divine Commander so will. There would be no need for an order, a look, a sign would be sufficient.

Ever since I came into Carmel I have pondered on the text, that if our Lord did not take me quickly to heaven, the lot of

Noah's dove would be mine. One day, opening the window of the Ark, he would command me to fly away to heathen lands, bearing the olive branch. This firm hope has enabled me to soar above earthly things. 'At the end of forty days, Noah opened the window he had made in the Ark. He released a raven, which flew back and forth as it waited for the waters to dry up on earth. He then released a dove to see whether the waters were receding from the earth. The dove, finding nowhere to perch, came back to him in the Ark, for there was water over the whole face of the earth. Putting out his hand, he took hold of it and brought it back into the Ark with him. After waiting seven more days, he again released the dove from the Ark. In the evening the dove came back to him and there, in its beak was a freshly picked olive leaf. So Noah realised that the water was receding from the earth. He waited seven more days and then released the dove, it never returned to him.' **(Genesis 8: 6–12)**

> **Meditate.** *Saint Therese, you are indeed the dove of the Ark of Carmel. You were released to soar in heaven and bring us the sign of peace. Jesus' sign to His entire Universe is Peace and this message is the message of the Little Flower. We ask that peace should rise up on the wings of prayer from our hearts. Saint Therese, you soar over the floodplains of this world and bring us back to the Ark of His Covenant, His new and everlasting covenant forged in the fire of His Sacred Heart, the flower of His sacrifice. You have the martyr's palm, little sister; pray for us that we bring, with you, the olive twig of peace in our hearts for Him.*

Knowing that even in Carmel, there must be partings, I have anticipated this separation by making my home in heaven. I have accepted in this attitude of prayer that I am an exile here in the midst of an unknown people. This was not done for myself alone but much for my sisters also. Two were asked for from our foundation, for the Carmel of Saigon and it was seriously considered. My heart ached at the thought of the trials that awaited them but I would not say a word to hold them here. All that is over now. Our superiors presented insurmountable obstacles, so that my lips tasted only the rim of the cup of sorrow.

Let me tell you, Mother, why if Our Lady cures me I want to respond to the call from our convent in Hanoi. It is apparent that a very special vocation is needed to live in the Carmels abroad. Many who believe they are called are mistaken, but you have told me I have this special vocation and that only my poor health stands in the way.

If one day I am obliged to leave the cradle of my religious life, it will be with an ache in my heart. For my heart is naturally sensitive and because it has the tender capacity for pain I offer to Our Lord every kind of suffering that it can bear. Here I am, loved by you and all the sisters and because this love is so sweet to me, I have a dream of a convent where I am unknown, where I should taste the bitterness of exile.

Meditate. *Our Lord was an exile here on earth from His home in Heaven, an exile among those who did not know Him. As a stranger He comforted them, suffered for them and died for them.*

Jesus, comfort us, your brothers and sisters that we go out into the world and give comfort to all we

> *meet. Then we truly shall be as you are a comforter*
> *and guide to all who are in need. Saint Therese, you*
> *teach us the little way and, as we are exiles here from*
> *our true home in heaven, comfort and guide us until*
> *He calls us home to heaven.* **Alleluia.**

I know very well of how little use I am. It would not be
then, for the sake of any service which I might render to the
Carmel of Hanoi. My only reason for leaving everything dear
to me would be to do God's will as a sacrifice of myself for
His goodness. I would not be at all disappointed, for when
we expect only suffering, the smallest joy comes as a great
surprise. When we seek suffering as His precious gift, then it
becomes the greatest of all joys.

I shall not recover from this illness. My soul nonetheless
abides in peace, for I have long since ceased to belong to myself.
I have surrendered my whole being to my Spouse and He is
free to do His pleasure. He has awakened in me the attraction
for a life of complete exile and He has asked me to consent to
drink of that chalice. Without any hesitation I tried to grasp it
but He, withdrawing His hand, showed me that my consent
was all He desired.

> **Meditate.** *Our consent, like the Patriarch Abraham,*
> *is our pledge to God that 'His will be done here on*
> *earth'. He stayed the hand of the Patriarch and*
> *provided the Ram for sacrifice. Thus we know that on*
> *His Holy Mountain, God provides.*

"O my God, we free ourselves from so much turmoil by the
vow of obedience! Happy is the simple religious, her only

guide is the will of her superiors, she is always sure that she is not misled even should it transpire that her superiors were mistaken. Should she ever cease to consult this unerring compass then, at once her soul would go astray into barren wastes where the waters of grace quickly fail. You, Mother, are the compass which Jesus has provided to direct me safely to the eternal shore. It is a joy to gaze upon you and to do the will of the Lord. By permitting me to suffer these temptations against faith, He has increased in me the 'Spirit of Faith', that faith which makes me see Him living in our Soul and communicating through you His holy commands. I understand that you make this burden of obedience sweet and light. Deep in my heart I feel that my attitude toward you would remain the same and my affection would be as great if you treated me with undue severity; for I would see the will of God made manifest in you as another way for the greater good of my soul."

Prayer

Meditation of Saint Therese

I no longer have any great ambition beyond that of living until I die of love.

It is God's love that holds us when we die, His love which cradles us in His incarnation so that in life He lives with us in love and draws us to that closer union, our spouse in death.

So we die of love and pass into a long embrace, the embrace of heaven, the home of holiness. We die here of love and come to eternal life drawn by His love in procession of the Holy Trinity.

When we pass away in love, we leave behind corruption and the fraying edges of decay. We die in love, the gateway to our Resurrection, Our Resurrection in Christ Our King.

He died for love of us and conquered death so that dying in His love is the way of life. To die in love is to enter into eternal life that from nothingness to creation, we rise up in life.

Love leads us from this pilgrim place. When love has ripened in our hearts, we die of love as the flowers of His pruning die. Dying of love is the only way into His arms. Dying of love is our consummation, Consumed into the flames of His Sacred Heart. Dying of love is far beyond material sensation. It is to live truly in incarnation, spiritual beings, inhabitants of the New Jerusalem.

understand how it is Christ in us that will do these wonders if only we open our hearts and obey His will.

O my Jesus, you never ask the impossible and you know better than I do how frail and imperfect I am. You know that I shall never love my sisters as you love them unless you love them yourself within me, my dearest Master. It is because you desire to give us this grace that you have given us this new commandment; dearly do I treasure it since it confirms to me that it is thy will 'to love in me' all those that you lead me to love.

> **Meditate.** *On the Mass*
> *The gift of His loving presence here with us confirms our faith for He justifies us in His Body and Blood, His life of sacrifice.*

Jesus 'loves in me'; this revelation to us through the Saint, of His loving presence in His faithful, illuminates the gift of Himself in the bread and wine consecrated for us in the Mass. The Eucharistic sacrifice both enables us and empowers us to live with Christ as Christ in us. Thus it is through faith that we merit His love and with His love bring His redemption and salvation to the world.

We might call this our justification by faith but this requires our active will to come before Him in His Church and practise our faith by this act of thanksgiving and consecration within His priesthood led by the High Priest Jesus in the brotherhood which He ordained must follow Him, His priesthood bound to Him in the Gospels.

We are redeemed and sanctified in His Sacramental presence, His Church by our merit in offering ourselves with

Him the perfect offering. Thus do we merit our justification by our life in Jesus the Christ and He in us. May the reformers be reformed and return to the Little Way of Love!

The Saint, our little sister, continues:

When I show charity towards others I know it is Jesus who is acting within me and it follows that the more clearly I am united in Him, the more clearly do I love my sisters. Should I wish to increase this love and then the devil appear to make me conscious only of her faults, then I go quickly in Christ and recall her many virtues and good intentions. I then recall that although I may have witnessed her fall once, she has surely gained many victories over herself, which in humility she has concealed. We remember also that what appears to be a fault may very well, as prompted by good intention, be an act of virtue. My own experience prompts me to recognise these hidden things in others.

One day during recreation, the Porter came and asked for help to complete a particular task. Now I had a childlike desire to do this very thing and it happened that I was chosen. I began to fold up my needlework slowly enough to allow my sister nearby to fold hers before me for I knew it would please her to take my place. The Porter saw my slowness and said mockingly, "I knew you would not add this pearl to your crown. You made sure of that!" All the community was given the impression that I had acted deliberately to avoid carrying out this menial task. I derived great profit from this incident and it made me feel compassion towards others. This curbing of the will keeps in check all feelings of vanity when I receive praise. I reflect that since virtue can be mistaken for imperfection, then imperfection may be mistaken for virtue.

Let us recall the teaching of St Paul (1 Corinthians 4: 3–4):

It is of no importance how you or any other human court may judge me. It is true that my own conscience does not reproach me, but that is not sufficient to justify me, it is the Lord who is my judge.

> **Meditate.** *'Judgement is mine says the Lord' and the Saint reminds us that as Saint Paul tells us, even our conscience is no sure guide in right judgement.*

Whatever the Law, human conduct is willed in act from personal subjective judgement. Our judgement as Christians is subject to God's judgement. Conscience is good and pure if it is inspired by faith and love, thus does the Saint rightly teach us that we can only truly achieve this when we let Jesus' 'love in me' be the spring-force of our will. For in this we are purified in the sacrifice of His blood which now lives in us through the sacrament of His Church.

Our little sister says: Since, therefore the Lord is my judge, I will always try to be compassionate of others, as He is my compassionate judge. Let me be no one's judge since He teaches, "Judge not, lest you also be judged" **(Luke 3: 37)**. Remaining with the Gospel, our Lord explains to me in what His new commandment consists. We read in Saint Matthew, "You have heard that it has been taught, 'You shall love your neighbour and hate your enemy.' I say to you, love your enemies and pray for them that persecute you". **(Matthew 5: 43, 44)**

There are of course, no enemies in Carmel, yet we have natural likes and dislikes. We may be drawn to one sister and in contrast, be tempted to go the long way round to avoid meeting another. Our Lord tells me that the sister I am tempted to avoid is the sister I must love and pray for, even though outwardly, she may give the impression that she does not care for me.

"If you love those who love you, what merit is there in this? Even sinners love those who love them." **(Luke 6: 30).** It is not sufficient to love passively because we should. We must prove and show our love through our actions. We take a natural delight in pleasing our friends but that is not charity, even sinners do the same. Elsewhere in the Gospels our Lord teaches me, "Give to everyone who asks and do not ask for your property back from someone who takes it." **(Luke 6: 30)** To give to everyone who asks provides less pleasure than giving spontaneously of one's own preference. Again if you are asked in a courteous manner, consent is easy; when tactless words are used we may often resist and rebel inwardly, unless we are perfect in Charity. We find no end of excuses for refusing and only after having made clear to the guilty sister how rude she is, do we grant begrudgingly, as a favour, what she requests. Or we render some trifling service which takes half the time which it has taken in explaining our justification of our own imaginary rights. It may seem difficult to give to everyone who asks, yet it is more difficult if anyone keeps our belongings that they have taken from us. I say this is difficult, but I should say that it only seems so for "the yoke of the Lord is sweet and His burden light". **(Matthew 11: 30)** When we put on that yoke we at once feel its sweetness. I said above that Jesus does not urge me to reclaim what belongs to me. This ought to occur quite naturally because in truth, I own nothing. Rather this practice is an occasion in which I should rejoice for it brings before me the understanding of poverty to which I am solemnly vowed. I used to imagine that I was detached from everything but now the Lord has revealed how imperfect I am. When I start to paint and I find the brushes in confusion or the ruler or penknife missing, I am tempted to lose my temper and I have to compel myself to resist demanding quite sharply for these articles I require.

Of course I may ask for them and I am not disobeying our Lord's command. In contrast I should be like the poor who hold out their hands for the necessities of life and when so often refused are not surprised because no one owes them anything. To rise above all social convention brings deepest peace, for there is no joy equal to that known by the truly poor in spirit. When they ask without expectation for something which they need and then are not only denied but deprived of what they have, they follow the Master's injunction, "If a man take away your jacket, let him have your overcoat as well". **(Matthew 5: 40)**

This means to me that to give up your overcoat is to renounce all rights and to know yourself as a servant, the slave of all. Without your greatcoat and jacket however, it is easier to walk or to run, so the Master adds, "If anyone require that you go one mile with him, go two miles." **(Matthew 5: 41)**

Therefore it is not sufficient for me to give to whomsoever asks. I must anticipate the request for service and when something set apart for me is taken, I should be glad to be rid of its burden.

> **Meditate.** *Blessed indeed are the poor in spirit for they have only the Love of God to bear them up and carry them away. Their poverty is the joy of freedom in Him. Blessed are the poor in spirit. They have given away all that holds them here. Their inheritance is the reality of His love born from above, this is borrowed*

time for them. The poor in spirit walk with God. They have listened to what is right. They love the Creator and Creation with compassion and in humility and obedience poverty is their friend.

I cannot always carry through this teaching of the Gospel, for sometimes I am compelled to refuse a request. Yet as Charity takes deep root in our souls, it is revealed, for when we refuse then it is with gracious longing and regret; this is a gift, reconciling us to the needy.

It is true that people are more ready to beg from those most ready to give. We must not then avoid the Sister in want because we do not have anything to give. The Master says, "Give to anyone who asks. When someone asks to borrow from you, do not turn away." **(Matthew 5: 42)**

I should not be quick to enhance my reputation, nor should I give in order to receive some favour. For it is written, 'If you lend to them from whom you hope to benefit in kind, what thanks are due? Sinners lend to sinners that it will be returned. Rather love your enemies and do good to them. Lend without thought of any return. Drive no one to despair of being in debt. You will have great reward; you will be children of the most High for He is kind to the ungrateful and the wicked'. On this road the first step alone is difficult, even here on earth the reward is great. To lend without thought of return may seem difficult. We are tempted to give outright for when we give something it is no longer ours. When a sister comes with our Mother's permission for a few hours' help, with the assurance that later on she will do the same for us, we may be certain that this will never happen and we are sorely tempted to say, "No, I will not lend it but I will give what you ask." Such a remark gratifies self-love; we are more generous in giving than lending! Our Sister then would know how little reliance we have for the promise. This is not the right practice of Charity. The divine precepts run counter to our natural inclinations. Without the help of grace it would not be possible to understand them and put them into practice.

I fear, dear Mother, that I have expressed myself more confusedly than usual. You will find nothing of interest in these rambling writings. I am not writing a work of literature and if I have wearied you by this discourse on Charity, you will still find in it evidence of your child's goodwill.

I confess that I am very far from living in the light of the teachings I have received, yet the desire to do so brings me peace. If I stumble in the practice of Charity, I immediately rise up again and for some months I have not even had to struggle. With our father, St John of the Cross, I have been able to say, "My house is at peace." This peace is the outcome of the victory I have celebrated over myself ever since the Hosts of Heaven have hurried to my aid to tend my wounds of my valiant fight on the occasion I shall now describe.

A holy nun of our community was a constant source of annoyance to me. The devil must have been involved, for without doubt it was he who made me see so many disagreeable traits in her character. I resisted this natural dislike of her and recalled that Charity must not only exist in the heart but also to show itself in deeds. I set out to treat this sister as my most cherished friend. Whenever we met, I prayed for her and offered God her virtues and merits. I knew that this would delight our Lord for there is no artist who is not pleased when his works are praised! The divine artist of souls is most pleased when we do not stop with the superficial but penetrate to that inner sanctuary which He has chosen as His dwelling place and admire its beauty. I was not content just to pray for this sister who was the occasion for me to demonstrate so much self-mastery. I set out to be of service to her whenever possible. When I was tempted to make her a disagreeable answer, I hastened to smile and changed the subject. "The Imitation of Christ" by Thomas a Kempis, says, 'It is more profitable to leave others with their thoughts than to enter into contentious discourses'. Sometimes, when the temptation was particularly strong, I would slip away without her realising my inward turmoil. I would run like a deserter from the battlefield. The result was that she said to me one day with a beaming countenance, "Tell me, Sister Therese, what is it that attracts you to me so strongly? Whenever we meet, you greet me with your most gracious smile."

What attracted me was Jesus hidden in the depths of her soul, Jesus who makes sweet even that which is most bitter!

> **Meditate.** *Lord, abide in us that we should see the mastery of your work in others. Our hearts are the sheepfold and our actions are like sheep. Restrain us and keep us close that we see your loving compassion in all mankind.*

I wrote, Mother, just now of my last resort for avoiding defeat, flight! It is scarcely an honourable tactic but whenever I took this course in my noviciate, it was always successful. I give you a notable example.

For several days you had been ill with bronchitis and we were all very anxious. One morning because I was the sacristan at the time, I entered your infirmary, very quietly, to replace the keys to the communion grating. Though I took care not to show it, I was inwardly happy that I would see you. One of the sisters was fearful lest I awake you and tried discreetly to take the keys from me. I told her very politely that I was as anxious as she that you should not be disturbed. I added that it was my duty to return them. I realise now that it would have been more perfect for me to yield. I did not think so at the time and I went to enter the room.

The noise awoke you and I was the cause of blame. This sister at length made the point that I was the guilty person. I was aroused with resentment and about to defend myself when it occurred to me that if I did so I would jeopardise my peace of mind. As I had not sufficient virtue to remain silent, I fled as the only path of safety. My heart beat so violently that I could not go far and I sat down on the stairway to savour in peace the fruits of victory. I understand that this is a perverse kind of courage yet preferable to certain defeat.

When I remember my days as a novice, I realise how far I was from perfection, though some things make me laugh. How good God has been to give my soul wings and train it to fly so freely! The hunter's net no longer frightens me for 'a net is spread out in vain for those with wings'. **(Psalms 1: 7)**

It may be that my current state, in future, will appear full of defects; nothing will surprise me. Nor does my helplessness and impotence distress me. I see glory in it and expect each day to detect more imperfections. It is so that this understanding of my nothingness does more good even than great revelations of matters of faith. I recall that 'charity covers up many sins' **(1 Peter 4: 8)**. I mine the riches of the Gospel, I trawl the deep of His immortal words and I cry with the Psalmist, "I have run in the stream of your command with a full heart which you give to me" **(Psalms 119: 32).** Charity alone widens my heart. O Jesus, I dash with delight in the way of your new commandment and I long to career along like this until the day of glory with your retinue of virgins. I follow you in the Kingdom, your Kingdom without end, singing the new canticle – the canticle of love!

God, in His infinite goodness has given me, dear Mother, a clear insight into the deepest mysteries of Charity. If I could express what I know you would hear heavenly music. I can however, only babble like an infant and without His own words to assist me, I would be tempted and hold my peace.

> **Meditate.** *Music unfolds the mystery of His love for music wells up from the heart like the ocean's swell. It is a double prayer for the sound of love is bound up in the harmony of His will and peace, that perfect resonance of pitch thrills through us and binds all creation in the harmony of the frequency of His perfect never-ending Love for all.*

The divine Master commands me to give to anyone who asks and binds me never to ask for what has been taken from me. This command holds here on earth and in heaven. For none of this is truly mine; I renounced the first in my vow of poverty and the other gifts I have on loan. If God withholds them I have no right to ask for them back! Nor should I complain. However, the fruits of our minds and hearts we regard as our own. We regard them as a personal sacred treasury upon which no one should lay a finger.

For instance, I pass on some light to a sister as though it were mine. When in recreation someone makes a witty comment which her neighbour repeats, without acknowledgement, to the community, its originator will regard it as a matter of theft. At the time she remains silent but at the first opportunity she will insinuate delicately that her thoughts had been borrowed!

Had I not been the perpetrator of all those human weaknesses, Mother, I would not be able to explain them. I should have preferred to believe myself unique in these petty temptations had you not bidden me to hear the novices' difficulties and give them advice. In the discharge of this duty, I have learnt much; above all I have been forced to practise what I preached.

I can only say in truth that by God's grace, I am no longer attached to the gifts of the intellect rather than I am to material things. Should any thought of mine please my sisters, I find it easy to let them regard it as their own. It belongs to the Holy Spirit, not me. Saint Paul teaches 'without the spirit of love, we cannot call God, our Father' **(Romans 8: 15)**. The Holy Spirit may use me as a channel to convey a good thought to a soul. That thought is not my private property.

We must not overvalue beautiful thoughts; even the highest aspirations are of little value without good works. Others may get profit from these lights provided they acknowledge them as grace from Our Lord, allowing them to share in the gifts to that privileged soul. Should that privileged soul take pride in her spiritual wealth, she imitates the Pharisee and becomes a person dying of starvation at a well-spread table, while his guests enjoy the rich fare and cast envious eyes on the possession of so many treasures.

How true it is that God alone can sound the heart. How myopic are His creatures. When they find a soul with insight that surpasses their own, they conclude that the divine Master loves them less! Yet when did He lose the right to use one of His children to provide others with the food they need? That right was not lost in the days of Pharaoh for God said to him, "Therefore I have raised you that I may show my power in you, that my name will be known throughout all the earth" **(Exodus 9: 16)**. Centuries have passed since these words were spoken by the Most High; His ways remain unchanged. He has always chosen human agents to accomplish His work among souls.

> *We are the work of His hands. All we are is His gift to us. Thus we follow untrammelled for His yoke is our perfection. Lord, we come to you in prayer; in your words we praise you. Your grace is our redemption, your never-ending love our Salvation. Walk with us, Our Saviour. Work in us, Our Redeemer. Journey with us, our heart's desire. Pray with us, our friend and master.*
>
> *Alleluia! Alleluia!*

all probability He will sleep on until my great and everlasting retreat.

This knowledge makes me rejoice rather than grieves me. Such a frame of mind is sufficient to show you that in truth, I am not a saint, for I ought not to rejoice in my dryness of soul but rather know it as a lack of fidelity and fervour! I suppose that I ought to be distressed that I so often fall asleep during meditation and thanksgiving after Holy Communion, but I recall that little children, asleep or awake, are equally dear to their parents and that to perform operations, doctors put their patients to sleep and most tellingly that 'The Lord knows our frailty, He remembers that we are but dust.'

Meditate. Preparation for Mass – The Prayer of Saint Thomas Aquinas

Almighty and ever living God, I approach the sacrament of your only begotten Son Our Lord Jesus Christ. I come sick to the Doctor of Life, unclean to the fountain of mercy, blind to the radiance of eternal light and poor and needy to the Lord of heaven and earth.

Lord, in your great generosity Heal my sickness, wash away my defilement, enlighten my blindness, enrich my poverty and clothe my nakedness. May I receive the bread of Angels.

The King of Kings and Lord of Lords With humble reverence And purity of faith And the repentance and love, the determined purpose That will bring me to salvation. May I receive the sacrament of the Lord's body and blood and its reality and power, Kind God.

May I receive the body of your only begotten son

Our Lord Jesus Christ Born from the womb of the
Virgin Mary And so be received into his mystical body
And numbered among his members.

Loving Father, As on my earthly pilgrimage I now
receive your beloved son Under the veil of a sacrament
May I one day see him face to face in glory Who lives
and reigns with you forever.

Amen*.*

The saint continues, "Yet apparently barren, my retreat and those which followed from them, I received unconsciously many interior beams of light revealing the best means of pleasing God and practising virtue. I have come to realise that Our Lord never gives me a full larder of provisions, but nourishes me piecemeal with food that is always new and fresh. I find it in my soul without being aware of how it got there. I believe in simplicity, that it is Jesus Himself hidden in my poor heart who is silently at work, inspiring me from moment to moment with whatever He wishes me to do".

"Just before my profession, I received the Holy Father's blessing through the kindness of Brother Simeon and I am certain that this precious blessing helped me through the fiercest storm of my entire spiritual life."

On the eve of that great day, usually so full of sweetness for a novice, my vocation came to be for me an unreality like a dream. The Devil for it was he, assured me that I was wholly unsuited for the Carmelite life and by going through with it, I was deceiving my superiors. The darkness became so dense that only one course of action was open to me; I had no vocation and must return to the world. I cannot describe my torment. What must I do in the face of such difficulty?

Happily, I chose the correct course and decided to tell our Novice Mistress about this temptation without delay. There and then I called her out of the choir and in my confusion, revealed the true state of my soul. Fortunately her insight was keener than mine – she laughed at my fears and reassured me. The Devil fled instantly at this humble avowal, he had tried to keep me from speaking and thus drawn me into his snares. Now it was my turn to ensnare him, so to complete my humiliation, I also told everything to Mother Prioress whose consoling words dispelled all the remaining shadow of doubt. Next morning, September the eighth, my soul was flooded with heavenly joy and in a state of tranquil 'peace which passes all understanding' **(Philippians 4: 7)**, I pronounced my holy vows. Many were the graces I asked and as I now truly was a 'Queen', I took advantage of my title to beg from the King all possible grace and favours for His ungrateful subjects. No one was forgotten. I longed and yearned for every sinner on earth, that they might be converted. I pleaded that all captive souls in Purgatory were set free, and on my heart I wore this letter containing all that I desired for myself.

The Prayer of Therese, the little Queen

O Jesus, my Divine Spouse, grant that my Baptismal robe may never be soiled. Take me from this world rather than allow me to stain my soul by committing the least wilful fault. May I never seek or find anything but Thee. May all creatures mean nothing to me and I nothing to them. May no earthly event disturb my peace.

O Jesus, I ask for peace, peace and above all love, love without limit. I ask that for your sake I may die a martyr; give me martyrdom of soul or body; more than this give me both.

Grant that I may fill my promises in all their perfection; that no one may think of me, that I may be forgotten and trodden underfoot as a grain of sand. I offer myself to you, O my Beloved that you may ever perfect in me Thy Holy Will, without your creatures placing any obstacle in the way.

Meditate. (Philippians 4: 6–7) *The Lord is near. Never worry about anything, but tell God all your desires of every kind in prayer and petition impregnated with gratitude and the peace of God which is beyond our understanding will guard your hearts and your thoughts in Christ Jesus.*

"May the smile and humility of gratitude be a mantle and cope on our shoulders.

For to be in you is to become like you, perfect in love for the Father and for all."

Saint Therese
From her letters

"When at the close of that glorious day, I laid my crown of roses, as was the custom, at Our Lady's feet, it was without regret. I felt that time could not steal this feeling of happiness.

Was not the feast day of the Nativity of Mary a beautiful day to become the spouse of Christ? It was the little newborn Mary who presented her little flower to the little Jesus. That day everything was little except the graces I received. My peace and joy, as I gazed up at the night sky, the glorious starlit sky, was profound. I thought that in just a little while I would take flight to heaven and there be united with my Divine Spouse in eternal bliss.

On September 24th, I received the veil but this feast was heavily veiled in sorrow. Papa was too ill to come and bless his 'little Queen' and at the last moment, Mgr Hugonin, who was to preside at the ceremony, was prevented from doing so; for other reasons too it was a day of gloom. Yet through all, my soul was at peace. It pleased Our Lord that on this occasion I should be unable to restrain my tears and they were not understood. True, I had borne far harder trials without shedding a tear, but on those occasions I had been buoyed up with special graces, whereas on the day of my veiling, Jesus left me to myself and I soon revealed my weakness. Eight days after taking the veil, my cousin Jeanne was married to Dr La Neale and at her subsequent visit, I heard of all the little attentions she lavished on her husband. I was greatly impressed and I determined it would never be said that a woman in the world did more for her husband than I for my Beloved. Filled with fresh ardour, I set out with increased vigour to please my heavenly spouse, the King of Kings, who had favoured me with the honour of a divine alliance."

When I saw the letter announcing our cousin's marriage, I thought to amuse myself by composing an invitation which I read to the novices in order to set before them what had been brought home to me – that earthly unions, however magnificent, are as nothing compared to the titles of alliance of a Spouse of Christ.

God Almighty, Creator of Heaven and Earth, Sovereign ruler of the Universe and the most Glorious Virgin Mary, Queen of the Heavenly Court, announce to you the Spiritual

Espousals of their august Son Jesus, King of Kings and Lord of Lords, with little Therese Martin, now Princess and Lady of His Kingdoms of the Holy Childhood and the Passion, assigned to her in dowry, by her Divine Spouse, from which Kingdoms she holds her titles of nobility, of the Child Jesus and of the Holy Face. It was not possible to invite you to the wedding feast, which took place on the mountain of Carmel, September 8th 1890. The heavenly court was alone, admitted, but you are requested to be present at the 'At Home' which will take place tomorrow, the Day of Eternity, when Jesus, the Son of God will come in the clouds of heaven, in the splendour of His majesty, to judge the living and the dead. The hour being uncertain, you are asked to hold yourselves in readiness and to watch.

I prepared myself during a fervent Novena for the retreat in the following year after my profession. I anticipated that it would be a year and a time of severe suffering. I often find preached retreats most trying, but this one proved an exception and brought me great graces. We had heard that the priest who was to give it understood much better how to convert the sinner than to direct nuns. If that were so, I must have been a great sinner since God made use of him to bring me such consolation.

I had previously been beset with all kinds of interior trials, which I found impossible to communicate to others. Now I unburdened myself in a simple straightforward manner so that the Priest understood me completely and he divined the state of my soul. He launched me full sail upon the ocean of confidence and love which had for so long attracted me but over which I dared not sail. He also told me that my faults did not grieve Almighty God. "At this moment," he told me, "I hold His place and be assured (that is the place of the Holy

Spirit) that I speak on His behalf. He is well pleased with your soul!" These comforting words filled me with joy for I was not aware that it was possible that faults should not give pain to God. This Father's assurance gave me patience to bear this exile. It was also the very echo of my innermost reflections. I had long known that Our Lord was most tender, more than any mother. Sadly, I have sounded the depths of more than one mother's heart. I know by sweet experience, how ready a mother is to forgive the small involuntary faults of her child. I remember how no reproach could have touched me more than one single kiss of forgiveness from you. Fear makes me shrink, while under love's sweet rule, I not only advance, I fly! Two months after this retreat, our Saintly foundress, Mother Genevieve of St Teresa, left us for the Carmel of Heaven. Before speaking of my impressions at the time of her death, I should like to tell you of the joy it was to have lived for some years with a soul whose Holiness was so sublime, subsisting in the practice of simple and hidden virtue. On many occasions, she brought me great consolation. One Sunday, when I went to see her in the infirmary, I found two of the elder nuns with her. As I was quietly retiring, she called me to her and said in an animated manner, "Stay, my child, you often ask me for a spiritual posy, today I give this to you. Serve the Lord in peace with joy. Recall always that our God is the God of Peace." I thanked her and left the room, moved to tears, convinced that God had revealed to her my state of turmoil, for I had been sorely tried that day, even to the verge of sadness. The darkness within my soul was so dense that I no longer knew if God loved me. You can understand how great was the light and consolation that came upon me.

The next Sunday, I asked Mother Genevieve if she had

a revelation concerning myself. She said she had not. This increased my admiration for her, for it revealed how intimately Jesus lived in her heart, directing every word and action. This is the degree of Holiness I aspire to, a holiness that is truly holy and free from any taint or illusion.

On the day that this dear Mother's exile ended, I received a very special grace. It was the very first time I had assisted at a deathbed and although the scene moved me deeply, I must confess that a kind of torpor crept over me. I was grieving at my insensitivity when at the moment she passed away, an extraordinary change swept through me. In an instant I was elated with an indescribable joy and fervour. It was as if the soul of our blessed foundress had made me a sharer in the happiness which she now possessed. I am certain that she went straight to heaven. One day sometime since I remarked to her, "You will not go to Purgatory, dear Mother." "I hope not," she replied most gently. I am assured that God would not disappoint so humble a trust. In the many favours we have received through her intercession, is the proof that her hope was fulfilled.

Each sister hastened to obtain something belonging to our Beloved Mother and you know the precious treasure which I cherish. During her agony, I noticed a teardrop glistening on her eyelash like a diamond. That tear, the last she shed here on earth, never fell. I saw it shining as her body lay in state in the choir. When evening came I went with courage, unseen and with a little piece of linen. I am now the happy possessor of the last tear of a saint.

I attach no importance to my dreams for they seldom have any meaning. Yet I wonder, how is it that since I think of God all through the day, that my mind does not invoke Him more when I am asleep? As a rule, I dream of woods and flowers, of brooks and the sea. I nearly always meet with pretty children or chase birds and butterflies which I've never seen before. My dreams are then sometimes practical but never mystical. One night after Mother Genevieve's death, I had a consoling dream. I saw her giving to each of us something which had belonged to her. When my turn came her hands were empty and I feared I was to receive nothing! Then she looked at me lovingly and said three times, "To you, I leave my heart." "To you, I leave my heart." "To you, I leave my heart."

Towards the end of 1891, about a month after that death, so precious in the sight of God, an influenza epidemic broke out in the Convent. I had only a slight attack and was able to go about with two other sisters. It is impossible to convey the heart-rending state of our Carmel during those days of mourning. The worst sufferers were nursed by some who could hardly stand upright. Death was all around us; no sooner had one sister breathed her last than we had to leave her and attend to another. My nineteenth birthday was saddened by the death of our sub-Prioress. With the infirmarian, I assisted at her last agony. Two more deaths followed in quick succession. During this time I did all the Sacristy work unaided and I wonder now how I found the strength.

One morning I had a presentiment that Sister Magdalen was dead. The corridor was unlit and in complete darkness, no one as yet had left her cell. I hastened to Sister Magdalen's cell and found her lying fully dressed upon the bed. I was not afraid and went quickly to the Sacristy and brought a blessed candle and placed a wreath of roses on her head. Amidst all this desolation, I felt the hand of God and I knew that His heart was watching over us. It was without a struggle that our dear Sisters left this life to enter into a happier one. They lay as if asleep with an expression of heavenly peace on their faces.

Throughout those trying weeks, I had the unspeakable joy of receiving Holy Communion every day. It was the sweetest grace. Jesus treated me as a spoilt child for a longer time than His most faithful spouses. After this epidemic, He came to me on a daily basis for many months, a privilege not shared by the community. I had not sought this favour but it brought me untold happiness to be united day after day to Him whom my soul loved.

I rejoiced in being able to touch the sacred vessels and to prepare the linen on which Our Lord was to be laid. I desired to increase in fervour and often recalled the words addressed to a saintly deacon, 'Be you holy, you who carry the Vessels of the Lord'.

Dear Mother, what can I tell you about my thanksgiving after Communion, not only then but always? There is no time when I have less consolation. This is not surprising because it is not my own satisfaction which I seek on receiving Our Lord, but solely to give Him pleasure.

Looking upon my soul as a piece of waste ground, I plead to Our Lady to take away my garbage, those heaps of rubbish, and to put up a spacious pavilion worthy of heaven and to make it beautiful with her own adornments. I next invite in all the Angels and saints to sing Canticles of love and I feel that Jesus is pleased to find Himself welcomed with such magnificence and then I too, share His joy. However this does not keep at bay the distractions and drowsiness and then I resolve to continue my thanksgiving through the day in amends for my neglect in Choir. You will note, dear Mother, that my way is not the way of fear. I can always find ways to be happy and to profit by my failings. Our Lord Himself encourages me in this. Once, in contrast to my usual state of happiness, I was troubled on approaching the Holy Table. For some days the hosts had been insufficient and I only received a small part of one. On this particular morning the foolish thought came to me, that if this happened again I must understand that Our Lord did not care to come into my heart. I approached the rails, for a moment the Priest hesitated, then gave me two entire hosts! What a loving response!

I have a great deal for which I am thankful to God, dear Mother, and I want to tell you something without guile. He has shown the same mercy to me as to King Solomon. All my desires are satisfied; not only desires of perfection but even those embedded in my vanity without bad intention. You have always been my ideal and I wanted to be like you in all things. You used to paint delightful miniatures, to write beautiful poems. This awakened in me a great desire to learn how to paint, to express my thoughts in verse for the edification of those around me. I would not ask for these natural gifts, so my wish remained dormant in my heart. Jesus, also hidden there, showed me the vanity of all things that pass away. To the surprise of many, I have succeeded in painting some pictures, in writing poems and in doing some good for certain souls. Just as Solomon 'turning to all the works of his hand and looking upon all his labours in vain, he saw in all these things vanity and vexation of mind'. Likewise, experience has taught me that the only happiness on this earth consists in remaining hidden in Him, in ignorance of created things. I understood that without love, even the most audacious of deeds counts as nothing. The gifts given to me by God drew my soul more closely to Him and made me grasp that He alone is unchangeable, that He alone can fill my vast longing for peace. My Divine Master has granted other more trivial desires like the wish for snow on my clothing day. Also, dearest Mother, you know how fond I am of flowers and that when I made myself a prisoner at the age of fifteen, I gave up forever the delight of walking through meadows bright with the treasures of Spring. Yet I never possessed so many flowers as are mine here in Carmel. In the world, young men present choice flowers to their betrothed. In like manner, Jesus did not forget me. I received for His Altar, an abundance of all the flowers I loved best, cornflowers, poppies, marguerites ... one little friend alone was missing, the purple vetch. I longed to see it again and just recently, it came to make me glad and to show the loveliness of the least as in the greatest. God gives a hundredfold even in this world to those who have left all things for love of Him.

The dearest of all my desires and the most difficult to attain, for many reasons, was my wish to see Celine enter the Carmel of Lisieux. I made a sacrifice of this and committed the care of my loved sister to God alone. I was willing that she would go to far distant lands if need be, but I wanted to see her like myself, the spouse of the Lord. I knew that in the world, she was exposed to dangers which I had never known. I suffered intensely, for my affection for her was that of a mother rather than a sister. I was filled with anxiety for the welfare of her soul.

One evening when she attended a dance with our aunt and cousins, I was more anxious than usual and I implored the Lord to intervene and prevent her from dancing. My prayer was heard and not only was His future spouse prevented from dancing but her partner as well. He had to walk up and down with her in all solemnity. This poor young man eventually slipped away, much embarrassed and was not seen again that evening. This incident proved clearly to me that Our Lord had already set His seal on Celine's brow.

On Sunday July 29th 1894, God called to Himself our saintly and much-tried father. During the two years prior to his death, he had lived in our uncle's house where he had the most tender care. Due to his debilitating condition, we saw him only once during the whole course of his illness. It was a sad meeting. You will recall, dear Mother, how at the parting moment, he raised his eyes and pointing upward, his voice choked in tears, he said, "In Heaven."

Now that he had reached that beautiful home, the last ties, which bound his consoling angel to the world, were severed. When angels have accomplished their mission here below, they take instant flight to God. Is not that the reason that they have wings? Celine also tried to fly to Carmel but the opposition she met on all sides seemed insurmountable. When matters were going from bad to worse, I said to Our Lord one morning after Communion, "You know, dear Jesus, how earnestly I have sought that my dear father's trials here should serve as his Purgatory. I long to know if this wish has been granted. I do not ask for a word, just a sign. You know that one of our community is strongly opposed to Celine's entry into Carmel. If she withdraws her opposition, I will regard it as an answer from you and in this way, I shall know if my father went straight to heaven."

God, who holds in His hands the hearts of His creatures and inclines them as He wills, deigned in His infinite mercy and ineffable condescension to change that sister's mind. After my thanksgiving, she was the first person I met. With tears in her eyes, she spoke to me of Celine's entrance, expressing a keen desire to see her amongst us.

Shortly after, the Bishop of Bayeux removed the last obstacle thus allowing you, dear Mother, without the least hesitation, to open the door of our Ark to the poor exiled dove.

Now I have no more desires except it be to love Jesus, even unto folly. Love alone draws me. I want neither suffering nor death, yet both are precious to me. I long to call to them as messengers of joy. Already I have suffered much; already it seems to me that my barque is nearing the eternal shores. From the earliest, I believed that the little flower would be gathered in her Springtime. Now the spirit of self-abandonment is my sole guide – I have no other compass. I am no longer able to ask for anything other than the accomplishment of His perfect designs upon my soul. I can now say these words of our Father, St John of the Cross:

> *I drank deep in the cave of my Friend. Coming out, I recognised nothing on this plain. I had lost the flock I once tended. My soul and all else I gave to Him. I no longer tend my flock; all my work is done. My only exercise now, is love alone.*
>
> *Love has changed me. Since I have surrendered to its power all within me, good or bad, serves only the end it seeks, transforming my soul into love itself.*

How sweet is the way of love. True one may fall and be unfaithful to grace but love knows how to draw profit from everything. It quickly consumes whatever is displeasing to Our Lord, leaving in the heart only a deep and humble peace. I have been much enlightened by the works of St John of the

Cross; between seventeen and eighteen, they were my only food. Afterwards I found all other spiritual writers leave me cold, they still do. However beautiful and touching a book may be, my heart does not thrill. I read without understanding or if I understand, I cannot meditate. In my helplessness, the Holy Scriptures and the Imitation are of the greatest comfort. I find in them the manna of heaven. It is however, from the Gospels that I derive most help in time of prayer. In their pages there is all that my poor soul needs and I am always able to find new illumination and the mystery of spiritual meaning. I know by this experience, that 'The Kingdom of God is within us'. Our Master needs no books or teacher to instruct our soul. The Teacher of Teachers instructs without the aid of sound or words. I have never heard Him speak yet I know He is within me, always guiding and inspiring me and as I need it, clarity of understanding hitherto unknown, breaks in upon me. As a rule, this happens not in prayer but in the midst of my daily duties.

Dear Mother, with so many graces, I sing with the Psalmist, 'the Lord is good, His mercy lasts forever'. If every soul received such favours God would be loved to excess and feared by none. I believe that every last wilful fault would be avoided out of love, without thought of fear.

Yet all souls cannot be alike. They must differ so that each Divine perfection may receive due honour. To me, He has manifested His Infinite Mercy and in this splendid mirror, I contemplate His other attributes, all perfect. There, each appears radiant with love, His Justice perhaps more than the rest. What a sweet joy to know that Our Lord is Just; that He takes into account our weaknesses and knows so well the frailty of our nature. What then need I fear? Will not God, of

Infinite Justice, who pardoned the Prodigal Son, be also just to me, 'Who is always with Him'? In the year 1895, I received the grace to understand better than ever how much Jesus desires to be loved. One day I thought of those who offer themselves as victims of the Justice of God, to turn aside the punishment due to sinners, taking that punishment on themselves. I felt such offering to be both noble and generous. I did not myself feel drawn to this action. From the depths of my heart I cried, "My Divine Master, shall your Justice only find atoning victims? Has not your merciful love need of them as well? On every side it is ignored and rejected. Those hearts, on which you would lavish it, turn to creatures instead. Seeking their happiness in the fleeting satisfaction of the moment rather than casting themselves into your arms, the ecstatic fires of your Infinite Love."

O my God, must this Love lie hidden forever in your heart? Is it not so, that if you should find souls offering themselves as holocausts to your love, you would consume them rapidly and be most pleased to set free those flames of infinite tenderness now imprisoned in your heart. If your justice, which avenges itself on earth, needs satisfaction, how much more must your merciful love desire to inflame such souls since, 'Your mercy reaches even to the Heavens'?

O Jesus, permit that I may be that happy victim. Consume your holocaust with the fire of Divine Love.

Dear Mother, who allowed me to offer myself to God, you know the flames of love, or rather the oceans of grace, which filled my soul when I made that 'Act of Oblation' on June 9th 1895. Since that day love surrounds and penetrates me. At every moment God's merciful love renews and purifies me, cleansing my soul from all trace of sin. I do not fear Purgatory

117

for I know that I do not deserve even to enter with the Holy Souls into that place of expiation. I also know that the fire of love is more sanctifying than the fire of Purgatory. Jesus could not will useless suffering for us and He would not inspire me with the desires I experience if He were not willing to receive them. This is all I can tell you, my beloved Mother, of the story of your little Therese. You know what she is and what Jesus has done for her, far better than she does herself, so you will forgive her for having greatly abridged this account of her religious life.

How will it end – this History of a little white flower?

Will she be gathered in all her freshness or will she be transplanted to other shores? I cannot say but this I know, that the Mercy of God will follow her everywhere and that she will forever bless the Mother who gave her to God. She will rejoice through eternity at being one of the flowers in that dear Mother's crown. I will sing together with her, the ever-new canticle of thanksgiving and love.

Alleluia! Alleluia!

CHAPTER 9

THE NOVICE MISTRESS

I F AN ARTIST'S CANVAS COULD THINK AND speak, surely it is certain it would never complain of being touched and retouched by the brush. It would not be envious of the brush for it would know that its beauty was the work of the artist. Neither could it boast of the masterpiece it had aided, for it would know that true artists overcome difficulties and to challenge themselves, they make use of the most unlikely and most defective instruments.

I am the brush our Lord has chosen to paint His likeness in the souls you have confided to my care. An artist will have of course, at least two brushes; the first which is most useful, provides the ground tints and covers the whole canvas; the second is a smaller one and is used only for details.

You, my dear Mother, are the valuable brush and our Lord uses it lovingly when He sets out to do great work in the souls of His children. I am the little one He uses afterwards to fill in the minor details.

It was on December 8th 1892 when the divine artist took up His little brush. I recall those days as a time of special grace. When I entered Carmel, I found a fellow noviciate who was eight years my senior. Despite this age difference we became close friends and to encourage this natural affection we were allowed, in order to foster virtue, to talk about spiritual subjects. My fellow novice charmed me with her innocence. She had a frank and open character, yet I was most surprised how her love for you differed from mine. In some ways her behaviour was a subject of regret. God had made me appreciate that there are souls for whom He waits in mercy. He never tires of giving them His light, little by little. I determined to wait upon His work.

One day, recalling the permission we had received to converse together so that we would, in accordance with our own Holy Rule, incite one another to a more ardent love for our Divine Spouse, I realised in sorrow that our conversations did not attain the required end. I realised clearly that either I must speak out fearlessly or I must end these conversations, for they were mere worldly talk. I begged our Lord to inspire me with kind words that would be convincing; better than this I asked Him to speak to her Himself instead of me.

He heard my prayer for, 'those who turn to Him shall be enlightened' **(Psalms 34: 5)**, and 'to the righteous a light arises from the darkness' **(Psalms 112: 4)**. The first of these texts applies to me, and the second to my companion who was truly upright of heart.

At our next meeting the poor little Sister understood straight away that my manner had changed; blushing deeply she sat down beside me. I spoke to her tenderly of the nature of true love. I revealed to her that in loving Mother Prioress with such natural affection, she was, in truth, simply loving herself. I told her of the sacrifices of this kind, which I had been obliged to make. Before long her tears flowed with my own.

She humbly acknowledged that she was wrong and acknowledged that what I had said was true. Then she asked as a favour that I would always point out her faults and vowed to begin a new life. From that day our love for one another became wholly spiritual and in us we fulfilled the words of the Holy Spirit, "A brother lifted up by his brother is like a strong city." **(Proverbs v. 18: 19)**

You must know, Mother, that I did not wish to turn my companion away from you. I set out to show her that true love is nourished by sacrifice and in proportion that we renounce natural satisfaction, our affections grow stronger and less selfish.

> **Meditate.** *Love seeks not to possess but to be possessed For love seeks unity not as object or subject But as one being without loss of identity so that though two persons, the loved and the beloved, belong to one another in the oneness of love the procession of love in the loved and the beloved is the movement in the Song of Songs*
>
> *The Lover loves the Beloved. The Beloved loves the Lover, thus they become love, one love that unites all. Myself, I'm lost in love to find myself, 'Beloved' in all. We are possessed in possessing the one we love.*

I recall that when I was a postulant, there were times when I was strongly tempted to seek my own satisfaction, a taste of pleasure in having a word with you. It was so strong an urge that I had to hurry past your door and cling to the banisters to keep myself from turning back.

I was tempted to seek permission for hundreds of different

things. I am glad that, from such beginnings, I learnt to practise self-denial. Now I enjoy the reward promised to those who fight bravely. Now I feel no need to refuse all consolations to my heart, for my heart is set on God. Because it has loved only Him, it has grown, little by little, so that now it can give to those who are dear to Him, far deeper love than if it were centred in a barren and selfish affection.

I have told you of my first piece of work, which our Lord accomplished, together with you, through His little brush. That was just a prelude to the masterpiece with which you entrusted it later.

From the time I first entered this sanctuary of souls, I realised that the task was beyond my strength. I took refuge in the arms of our Lord. I was like a child who, when frightened, buries its face on its Father's shoulder.

"You see, Lord, I am too small to feed your little ones," I cried, "therefore, give me that which is suitable for each one and in the shelter of your arms without turning, my Lord, I will distribute your treasures to those souls needing food. When I see them delight in it then I shall know that they owe it not to me, but to you. If they complain and find fault I shall persuade them that it comes from you and then take care that it comes from none other. "

This knowledge that I could do nothing of myself greatly simplified my task. I was confident that my one aim should be to unite myself ever more closely to God. All the rest would then come to me in abundance. Each time I needed food for the souls in my charge, I always found that my hands were full. Had I relied on my own powers I should very soon have been forced to give up.

In theory, it seems easy to be a shepherd to souls, to lead them to love God more and to pass on one's own insights and ideas. When we set to with this work we soon appreciate that without God's help it is impossible. It is like bringing back the sun once it is set. We must put aside our own ideas and step outside our own understanding. We must guide souls only along the paths which our Lord Himself shows us. The greatest difficulty, however, and for which we pay a heavy price, is that we are compelled to notice all their faults and the smallest imperfections and then wage war against them. I was going to say, 'unhappily for me', but that would be too cowardly! So I will say, 'happily for my novices', ever since I flung myself into the arms of Jesus I have been like a watchman on the lookout for the enemy from the highest turret of a fortified castle. Nothing escapes me; my clear-sightedness is most surprising and I believe it quite excusable for the prophet Jonah to have fled before the face of the Lord rather than announce the ruin of Nineveh. I prefer to receive a thousand reproofs rather than inflict one. Yet I know it is necessary that this task should cause me pain, for if I spoke from my own point of view, the soul at fault may not understand the fault but would think that 'the sister in charge of us is annoyed about some other matter and vents her displeasure on me, although I am not at fault'.

> **Meditate**. *Teach us, Lord, to offer up our thoughts that in their place we know your will. May our tongues be still that we might listen more. For out of the mouths of babes in arms you teach us the wisdom of your ways. Saint Therese, come and lead us home along the pathway of His loving arms. Come to us,*

Saint Therese; come that we should follow as you skip
along those pathways to our Father's home.

In this, as in all else, I must practise self-denial. When I write a letter I feel it will produce no fruit unless it costs effort, be it only out of obedience. So too, when talking to a novice I am always on watch to mortify myself. I avoid all questions which would only gratify my curiosity. Should she begin on an interesting subject and digress, I am careful not to remind her of her digression, for no good can come from self-seeking.

Your little lambs find me severe. I know, Mother, if they were to read these lines they would say, that as far as they are concerned, it does not appear that I am the least distressed to pursue them and then point out how they have soiled and torn their pure white fleece. Whatever they may say, they must know in their hearts that I love them with a very great love. I will not imitate the hired man, 'who when he sees the wolf coming, leaves the sheep and flees'. **(John 10: 12)**

I am ready to lay down my life for my novices, though my affection is so great that I would not let them know it. With God's help I have avoided the temptation that they should set their hearts on me. My mission has always been to lead them to Him and to you, Mother, you who on earth hold His place in regard to them. It is you therefore, they must love and respect.

I have already told you how much knowledge I gained from guiding others. All souls, I know, have more or less the same battles to fight but as two souls are never exactly the same I was aware that I must treat each individual differently. With some I need to humble myself and tell them of my own struggles and defeats. They then have less difficulty in acknowledging their own faults, consoled that others have these same difficulties. In dealing with others, my only hope of success is in being firm and never going back on what I have said, for this would be taken as a weakness on my part. Our Lord has given me grace never to fear conflict and to do my duty no matter what the cost. More than once it has been said to me, "If you want to do anything with me, treat me gently, you will gain nothing in being severe." No one however, is a good judge of their own case. During a painful operation children will cry out, say that the remedy is worse than the disease. Yet how great their delight after some few days, when they find that they are cured and able to run about and play. The same thing happens with souls; they soon recognise and confess that sternness is preferable to much sweetness and light.

The change, which takes place in a soul from one day to another, is sometimes really marvellous. "You did well to be severe with me yesterday," a novice said to me, "at first I was indignant then after some thought I knew you were right. I left your cell thinking that all was at an end between us and I determined to have nothing more to do with you. Then I became aware that these thoughts were from Satan and that you were praying for me. Gradually I became tranquil, the light began to shine and now I have come back to listen to all you have to say."

I was relieved and too happy to follow the dictate of my heart and I gave her food more tasty to her palate. Soon I found that I must not go too far lest a single sentence should bring down the edifice that had cost so many tears to build. If I let pass the slightest remark that would soften the hard truths of the previous day, my little sister would be quick to take every advantage. Then I had recourse to prayer; I turned to our Blessed Lady and Jesus was victorious. My entire strength lies in prayer and sacrifice; these are my invisible weapons. Experience has shown me that the heart is won by them rather than by words.

It was two years ago during Lent; a novice came to me with a radiant face. "You would never guess what I dreamed last night. I thought that I was with my sister who is very attached to worldly things. I wanted her to withdraw from such vanities and I explained to her these words of your hymn:

> *'Their loss is gain who give up all to find your love,*
> *O Jesus mine. For you my ointment jar I break, the*
> *perfume of my life is yours.'*

"I felt that what I had said had sunk deep into her heart and I was overjoyed. This morning it seems to me that Our Lord wants me to give Him this soul. Would you approve of my writing to her at Easter telling her of my dream and that Jesus desires her as His spouse?"

I told her that she most certainly could ask for such permission. Lent was not yet over and you were surprised at such a request. Inspired by God, you replied that Carmelites should save souls by prayer rather than by letter. Having heard your decision, I said to my little sister, "We must set to and work very hard at our prayers. What a joy it will be if our prayers are answered by the end of Lent."

Infinite mercy of God, by the close of Lent, one more soul had consecrated herself to God by a miracle of grace wrought by the fervour of a humble novice. The power of prayer is indeed most wonderful. It is like unto a Queen who having free and unfettered access to the King, can obtain whatever she asks. To secure a hearing you do not need to say special prayers composed for such a meeting. Was this the case, I would be pitied in my failing.

The Divine Office, despite my unworthiness, is a daily joy but I do not have the stamina to search through books for beautiful prayers. There are so many that my head would ache in choosing because each one is lovelier than the other. As I am unable to say them all or choose between them, I do as a child would who cannot read, I say in simplicity, just what I need to say and He never fails to understand me. This is what prayer is for me, it is an uplifting of the heart, a cry of gratitude and love in times of both sorrow and joy. It is something noble and supernatural which magnifies the soul and unites it to God.

When my spirit is so arid that not one single good thought comes to mind, I say very slowly, the Our Father and the Hail Mary, then I am consoled they are divine food for my soul.

Where am I? Once again, lost in a maze of reflections. Forgive me, Mother, for wandering off in this way. I am aware that my story is like a tangled skein of wool but it is the very best that I can do. My heart is like a lake into which I cast my net at random. Then I write down my thoughts as they come to me.

I was talking about novices. They often say to me, "You have an answer for everything; we really thought that we should catch you out this time. Where do you find all the things that you teach us?" Some are even ingenuous enough to believe that I can read their minds because on some occasions, I anticipate without prior knowledge, the subject of their thoughts!

On one such occasion a senior novice was determined to hide from me a great sorrow that was causing her much pain. She had spent a miserable night but had kept back the tears lest they betray her. When she came to me she was bright and cheerful and she spoke in a light-hearted way. I said to her, in simplicity, "I am sure you are in trouble." She stared at me in amazement, her surprise so great that it had an immediate impact on me, giving me an impression of the supernatural. I felt that God was there close to us and that unknowingly – for I do not have the gift of reading souls – I had spoken as one inspired. After this I was able to console her completely.

Now, dear Mother, I will tell you of my greatest spiritual gain when dealing with novices. You know that they are under no restriction and that they can say anything they want to say to me. This is as it should be since they do not owe me the respect due to a 'Novice Mistress'. I cannot say that our Lord makes me to walk humbly; He is content with humbling my inmost soul. In the sight of creatures, success crowns all my efforts. If the words may be used of life in the cloister, I walk upon that dangerous pathway of honour. In this I understand the design of God and my Superiors. If I were looked upon by my sisters as a useless member of the community both incapable of action and wanting in good judgement, you could not employ me to help you. Therefore, the divine Master has thrown a veil over my faults, interior and exterior. Many compliments come to me from the novices as a consequence. These compliments are sincere, for they mean what they say but I remember always my weakness, its presence is always with me so that there is no place for vanity. My soul sometimes tires of all this sweet food and longs for something other than praise. Our Lord serves me with a sharp salad, well mixed with vinegar, without oil that makes it much more to my taste. At times when I least expect it my novices set it before me. Lifting the veil, which hides my faults, God shows me to them as I really am. They do not then find me at all to their liking. With a directness that is delightful, they tell me how much I try them and what they dislike in me. In fact, they are so frank that it was as if I was not there. For they know that it pleases me when they are so outspoken.

This delicious banquet does more than please me; it fills my soul with Joy. How can anything so contrary afford such pleasure? Had I not experienced it I could not have believed it possible.

Once when I had an intense longing to be humble a young postulant granted my desire so aptly that I recalled the occasion in Holy Scripture when Semie cursed David. I recited the Holy King's words, "Yes, it is the Lord who has commanded him to say these things **(2 Samuel 16: 10)**. This is how God cares for me. He does not give me encouragement of exterior humiliation; instead I eat the crumbs from the table of the impoverished." How magnificent are his mercies.

As infinite mercy is the theme of the song I sing here on earth, dear Mother. I will tell here of another blessing I reaped from the discharge of my little task. In the past, when I saw a Sister breaking our Rule, I was glad to warn her and show her, her mistake. Now that it has become my duty to find and expose fault, I have changed my mind. When I by chance see something amiss, I sigh with relief, thanking God that the guilty one is not a novice and that therefore, it is not my business to correct her. Instead I do all I can to excuse her and to credit her instead with good deeds that no doubt she possesses.

Your devotion to me whilst I was ill, dear Mother, has taught me many lessons of charity. No remedy was too costly and should it fail, you tried something else. When I attend recreation you take every precaution to protect me from a chill. This care provokes me to feel compassion for the spiritual infirmities of my sisters. I have noticed that it is the holiest nuns who are most loved. All seek their company and seek to do them some service without being asked. Virtuous souls who do not seek any reverence find themselves both loved and revered. Our father, St John of the Cross, uttered a great truth when he said, "All good things have come to me, since I no longer seek them myself."

Imperfect souls, in contrast, are isolated and shunned. They are accorded politeness which the religious life demands but intimacy is avoided lest a careless word might hurt their feelings. I am not telling of spiritual imperfection for we are all blemished, I am referring to those who are insensitive and wanting in tact and refinement and make life unpleasant for others. These defects are incurable but I know how patient you are in nursing me even when my illness lasts for years. From these lessons I conclude that I ought to seek the companionship of Sisters for whom I have this aversion. Instead I try to be their Good Samaritan. Often it requires only a kind word or a smile to raise the spirits of a despondent companion. It is not in hope of bringing consolation that I am kind. For very often well-intentioned words are misunderstood. Consequently, in order that I do not lose time or labour in vain, I try to act only to please Our Lord as the Gospel teaches.

(Luke 14: 12–14, Matthew 6: 4) He said to His host, "When you give a dinner or supper, do not ask your friends or your brothers or your colleagues or even your rich friends, for they may send you invitations in return so that you will be recompensed for your hospitality. Rather, in giving hospitality, invite the poor, the crippled, the lame and the blind. Then you will win a blessing for they cannot invite you in return. Then your reward will come when the just will rise again."

I can only offer my sisters the spiritual feast of sweet and joyful charity. There is no other way and I will imitate St Paul who rejoiced with those who rejoiced! He also wept with those who wept and at the feast I give, tears must sometimes fall but I will always do my best to change them into smiles for God loves a cheerful giver **(2 Corinthians 9: 7).** I recall an act of charity when I was a novice through which God inspired me.

Although it was small to some, it has been richly rewarded in this life by our heavenly Father 'who sees all in secret'.

It was like this. Before Sister Peter became quite helpless, someone had to leave the evening meditation at ten to six and take her to the refectory. She was very difficult to please, this poor invalid, and it cost me greatly to offer my services. I did not want to let this opportunity pass, remembering Our Lord's words, "As long as you did it to the least of my brothers, you did it to me". **(Matthew 25: 40)**

I therefore offered my help and it was accepted, though only after considerable persuasion. Every evening when she shook her hourglass it was the signal to start. (In the spirit of poverty, the hourglass was used instead of a watch in the convent at this time.) Summoning up courage I rose and quite a ceremony began. First her stool had to be moved and carried in a particular way, and then the journey could begin without any hurry. Holding the poor old sister by her girdle, I tried to assist her as gently as possible. If she stumbled she told me sharply that I was going too fast and was trying to make her fall. Then, when I tried to lead her more slowly and gently, she would say, "Where are you, I can't feel your hand. You're letting go so that I'm going to fall. I knew you were too young to take care of me."

At last we reached the refectory, then fresh problems would arise. Taking every care not to hurt the poor invalid, I had to manoeuvre her into her place and then turn back her sleeves, always according to her special way, then I was free to go. I saw however, that she was having extreme difficulty in cutting the bread. I would not go until I had done this last service. As she had not asked me to do this she was greatly touched. Then I smiled sweetly and this won her entire confidence. This happened long ago but it lingers in my memory and Our Lord bestows upon me the perfume from heaven. One cold winter's evening when I was humbly leading Sister St Peter, there came to my hearing strains of distant harmonious music. A vision appeared before me of a sumptuously furnished room full of elegantly dressed young girls talking in a worldly fashion. Then I turned to the invalid and instead of sweet music I heard her grumbling complaints, instead of rich decoration there was the bare brick walls of our cloister, scarcely visible in the dim flickering light. The contrast thrilled me; my soul was illumined by Our Lord with the rays of His truth. In this light, the pleasures of this world are darkness. Not for a thousand years of such worldly pleasure would I have exchanged ten minutes spent in my act of charity. Now in pain in the smoke of battle, the knowledge that God has withdrawn us from the world is enchanting. What will it be like when in eternal glory and everlasting repose, we realise the favour He has done us here, in selecting us to dwell in His house which is the very porch of heaven?

Meditate. *Our Lord has given us our brothers and sisters to love instead of Him.*

These transports of joy do not always accompany my acts of charity. However, from the outset in the religious life, Our Lord made me to understand how sweet it is to see Himself at the heart of His spouses. Therefore, when I acted as guide to Sister St Peter, it was with the same love as if I had been leading Our Lord Himself. To show you some proof of my many difficulties, dear Mother, I shall relate some of my many struggles.

For a long time, my place in meditation was close to a Sister who fidgeted incessantly, either with her rosary or something else. Possibly, only I heard because of my sensitive hearing. I cannot tell you how much I was tried and irritated by this constant noise. I was strongly tempted to turn round and with a frosty glance silence the offender, yet in my heart, I knew that I ought to bear with her patiently. Firstly, for the love of God and also to avoid causing her pain. I remained quiet but the effort cost me greatly; sometimes I was bathed in perspiration and my meditation consisted only of the prayer of suffering.

Finally, I found a way of getting peace in my heart; I tried to find pleasure in this disagreeable noise. Instead of attempting not to hear it, I began to listen intently as though it were delightful music and my prayer of quiet became a prayer offering this music to Our Lord.

On another occasion when I was working in the laundry, the sister opposite, who was washing dirty handkerchiefs, kept splashing me with dirty water. My first impulse was to step back and wipe my face in order to show her that she should be more careful. However, I saw the folly of refusing such treasure so generously offered and I hid my annoyance. Instead I made every effort to welcome these showers of dirty water. After half an hour I had taken quite a fancy to this very novel immersion and resolved to return to this place where such precious treasures were to be freely bestowed.

You see, Mother, I am a little soul who can only offer God very little things. I still miss many opportunities of welcoming these small sacrifices which bring so much peace. I am not discouraged, I will be more watchful in the future.

How happy Our Lord makes me, how sweet and easy is His service in this life. He gives me all I desire or rather He has made me desire what He wishes to give. A short time before that terrible temptation against faith, I had been thinking how free I was from great outward trials and that only interior suffering was to be my lot.

God alone could alter my spiritual path and that did not seem likely. I knew that I could go on living in peace and quiet and wondered how God would act. The answer soon came and it revealed to me that He whom I love is never at a loss to give me greater things. For without pushing me aside, He sent me this great trial; which soon mingled salutary pain and bitterness with all the joy.

> **Meditate.** *God guides us and shares with us all His love. The pain and sacrifice of His life here, He shares with us, so that His Salvation is shared and can come to all. As the agony of Christ leads to His resurrection, may our sacrifices be received as worthy offerings through Him. Lord, in your mercy, hear our prayer.*

CHAPTER 10

THE PRAYER OF HUMILITY

HERESE, OUR SISTER, FLOWER OF HIS HEART, counsels us as her novices and they that had the joy of living in her company remember some of her words and works. These reminiscences are brought together from conversations with her sister novices, but the advice she gave is of universal merit as the Church acknowledges, in creating her in the honour, for us, of Doctor of the Church.

Speaking to a despondent novice who easily gave up at the thought of her failures in achieving the perfection of holiness, the Saint taught her novice and teaches us: You remind me of a little child beginning to learn how to stand up and already determined to climb the stairs in order to find your mother. Time and time again, the baby tries to lift its tiny feet up to the first step and each time it flops down and rolls over. You must do what that little baby does.

By diligent practice of all the virtues, keep on lifting your foot to clamber onto that first step in order to climb the ladder of perfection. Do not believe or imagine that you can, by yourself, succeed even in mounting the very first step. God asks of you only your goodwill. From the top of the stairs, the ladder of perfection, He gazes down on you most lovingly. Soon moved by your devotion and touched by your frustration, He will pick you up in His arms and take you to His Kingdom never to be separated from Him again. If you stop lifting up your foot, you will stay rooted to the ground and you will remain earthbound for a long time.

You must remain small, 'keep little', in order to make rapid progress on the pathway of divine love. This is what I have done so that now I can sing with our holy father, St John of the Cross, 'God places the treasure trove of all the virtues into the tiny hand of His little child so that He may use these treasures as He needs. It is a love gift, for these treasures belong to God'.

Finally, by remaining like little children, we shall not lose courage at the sight of our faults. Little children often tumble over but they are too small and supple to suffer grievous injury.

This is what the Little Flower wrote to one of her novices during a retreat:

Never fear or fail to tell Jesus that you love Him even though you do not actually feel that love for Him. In this way you will compel Him to come to you and carry you like a little child who is too weak to walk.

When a gloom settles and all is blackness, it is indeed a heavy cross to bear. You are not alone bound up in yourself. Try your hardest to detach yourself from worldly cares, especially from attachments to people and pets. Then rest and be sure that Our Lord will do all the rest. He could never allow you to fall into the abyss. Be strong and encouraged, good child! In heaven there is no darkness, everything will be illuminated in dazzling white, bathed in the Divine radiance of our Spouse, the pure, pure white Lily of the Valley. Together we will follow Him wherever He goes. In the meanwhile, we must make every good use of our lives here below. Let us give Our Lord things that please Him, let us, by our self-sacrifice, give Him souls! Above all let us remain small, so tiny that everyone can tread upon us without their knowing, as if we suffer no pain.

My little one's failures are not surprising. She sometimes forgets that she is both a missionary and a warrior and she should therefore give up all childish consolations. It is a very great folly to pass time fretting instead of resting peacefully and quietly on the Heart of Jesus. Nor should my 'little one' be at all afraid of the dark, nor complain that she does not see the Beloved, because it is He who carries her in His arms. She has only to close her eyes; this is the one sacrifice God demands of her. If she obeys Him in this, the dark will lose all its terrors because she will not be conscious of it and then very soon peace, if not joy, will return once more.

To help a novice accept, with goodwill, a particular penance of humility, she confided in her a resolution of her own.

"If I had not been accepted and received into Carmel I should have entered a Refuge [for the poor, the destitute, especially aged prostitutes often suffering from venereal diseases] and I would have lived there unknown and despised among the poor penitents. My joy would have been to pass among them and to be accepted as one of them. I should have become an apostle to them, telling them my thoughts on the infinite mercy of God."

The novice asks her, "How could you have hidden your innocence from your confessor?"

The Saint tells us, "I should have told him that whilst I was still in the world, I had made a general confession and that it was forbidden that I should repeat it.

"Oh, when I recall how much I had to acquire or in truth how much I had to lose. Jesus Himself fills our souls with goodness as we jettison all our imperfections. It is quite clear to me that you have taken the wrong road, it leads nowhere; you will never arrive at the end of your journey. Your aim is to climb to the top of the mountain – there is nothing there. God, you see, wishes you to climb down. He is waiting for you below in the verdant and fruitful valley of humility.

"To me it is clear that humility is truth. I do not know whether I am humble but I know that I see the truth in all things."

> **Meditate.** *In knowing the truth of created things we become aware of our own fragile smallness. In truth the magnificence of His Creation shines forth and we are astounded. Its immensity and beauty confirm our littleness. We look back from the moon in awesome wonder. The heavens engulf us in the immensity of order. We are amazed at the power in the minute atom. Truth humbles and raises us up. It holds up the mirror of our dependence in the Creator's Creation, of our humbleness. Truth and humility raise us up. From the dust heap from which we were made to behold the lily of the fields as stewards for Him. Humility forgives all for it has no claim. Humility is blind, clothed in Wisdom's blue gown. With our Little Sister who leads, we clap our hands with joy and sing of the little ones, the humble in heaven as the truth of His teaching on the Mountain of Blessings.*
>
> *Alleluia! Alleluia!*

It was said of Saint Therese, "Indeed, it is obvious you are a Saint!"

She replies, "No, I am not a saint. I have never wrought the works of saintliness. I am a very tiny soul whom almighty God has loaded with many favours. The truth of these words which I say will be made known to you in heaven."

The novice says, "But have you not always been faithful and loaded in favour?"

"Yes, from the age of three I have never refused Almighty God anything. Yet I cannot boast. You see how on this evening the tree tops are gilded by the setting sun, so too my soul appears to you all golden and shining only because it is exposed by the rays of Love. Should the Divine Sun no longer shine, it would sink immediately into gloom!"

The novice, like us, said, "We too would like to become all golden, burnished with the light of His love. What must we do?"

You must practise the virtues in the smallest ways constantly. This will sometimes be most difficult because they are easily overlooked but God never withholds the first and greatest grace, courage and resilience for self-conquest. When you respond positively to that grace, you will immediately find yourself in God's sunlit presence.

The praise given to Judith came home to my heart: 'You have done this with your own hand and your heart has been strengthened'.

> **(Judith 15: 11)** *'By doing all this with your own hand you have deserved well of Israel and God has approved what you have done. May you be blessed by the Lord Almighty in all the days to come.'*

The Saint sums up: "In the outset we must act courageously. In this way, the heart gains strength and victory follows on from victory."

Saint Therese never raised her eyes at mealtimes. She composed this prayer for those of us who find great difficulty in observing this rule of her little way.

Prayer of fragile humility

Jesus, for your sake remembering the example you gave us in the house of Herod, we your spouses resolve to keep our eyes cast down when we sit down to eat.

When that impious King mocked you, O Infinite Beauty, you made no complaint, remaining silent. You did not favour him with your adorable compassionate gaze but we, your spouses, long to be drawn into your divine eyes that you should look upon us with love. Whenever we keep our eyes downcast, we ask you to reward us with a glance of love and ask boldly that you should not refuse us this sweetest consolation even when we fail in our self-control for we humble ourselves most sincerely before you.

As novices, we confide in her that we make no progress and that, in consequence, we lose heart.

"Until the age of fourteen," she said, "I practised virtue without tasting its sweetness. I desired suffering for His sake but I did not think of making it my joy; that grace was given to me later. My heart and soul was like a beautifully splendid tree, the blossom opened and it fell straight away.

"Offer to God the great sacrifice of never gathering any

fruit from your tree. If it is His will that throughout your life you should feel repugnance to suffering and humiliation, if He allows the flowers of your desires and of your good deeds to fall without fruiting, do not worry. At the hour of death, in the twinkling of an eye, He will cause rich fruits to ripen on the tree of your soul."

> **Meditate.** *Suffering is like the swelling, growing pains of pollination. Sapping the tree of energy and vitality, making it work ever harder for the moment of separation in new life and new growth, life rising from death, anguish and deprivation. From the cold block of the trenching tomb, life rises up to greet the Son of Man.*

We read in the Book of Ecclesiasticus, "There is an inadequate person, without possessions, rich in poverty. Yet the Lord favours him and lifts him out of his wretchedness. This enables him to hold his head high. Many wonder at this and glorify God. Trust in God, the Blessing of the Lord is the reward of the devout. Stay in your place at prayer. It is easy for God to make a poor man rich. The Blessing of God is the reward of the just and in a passing moment His Blessing bears fruit". **(Ecclesiastius Ben Sira 11: 12, 13, 22–24)**

Still novices, we say, "If I were to fall, I shall always be found Imperfect, whereas you are Holy."

Our sister teaches, "Perhaps I appear holy because I have never desired to be considered holy. It is better for you to be found imperfect. This is your chance to gain merit. To believe oneself imperfect and others perfect, this is true happiness. Should others here on earth perceive you as lacking in virtue, then they can rob you of nothing. You cannot be poorer in their sight; it is they who lose. For there is no greater joy than believing well of your neighbour. As for myself I am glad and rejoice not only when I am seen as imperfect but most especially when I know it to be true. Compliments on the contrary, displease me and discomfort me."

We novices say, "God has a special love for you since He gives our souls into your care."

"That is of no consequence because I am only what I am to Him. It is not because He wills me to be His interpreter among you that shows that He loves me more; on the contrary, He makes me your little handmaid. It is for your sake and not for mine that He bestows upon me signs of virtue which you see. In contrast, I think of myself as a little stone bowl filled by God with good things. All the little kittens come to eat out of it and they squabble as to who should have the greater share. The Holy Child, Jesus keeps watch. 'I am willing,' He says, 'that you should eat from my little bowl. Be careful that you do not upset and break it.'

"In reality, there is no real danger because He keeps me on the ground. This is not so with Prioresses, set up on a high table; they are at much greater risk. Honour is always a danger. Poisonous food is served daily to those in high positions. What deadly fumes are those compliments rising like incense? A soul must be completely detached from herself to pass through it all without being scarred."

> **Meditate.** *The scent of blossom lifts our prayers In the prayer He gave to His creation. A perfume rising up to greet Him, Jesus coming on the clouds of mercy. The Holy Face is salvation's blossom, the sign of Glory*

dwelling here with us. The child Jesus at home in His Father's house. Let us play with Him and skip with Him, children of the light in this time of redemption. The holy face draws us up to heaven. The light of His gaze is our heart's splendour, Where the heart leads our feet follow, pilgrims on the joyful journey to our Father. Saint Therese, paint the scene for us Of snow and rain and sunlit meadows And trace the rose of England on His heart That in perfumed ranks we will follow Him to glory. Saint Therese, the Child of Jesus, sing His praise. Teach us to sacrifice in the little way of love.

BWF

We novices said to our sister, the Saint, "It is a consolation for you to do good and give glory to God. I wish we were equally favoured."

"It is of no importance if God makes use of me, rather than another way, to secure this glory! God has no need of anyone, provided His Kingdom is established here amidst His people. The instrument of His purpose is not important.

"Not long ago I was watching the flicker, almost imperceptible, of a tiny night-light. It happened as one of the sisters came in and having lit her candle in the dying flame, passed it on to light the candles of the others with her. The thought came to me, 'who dare glory in their own good works?' It needs just one faint spark to set the whole world ablaze. We come into the light touched with burning and shining lights set high on the candelabra of the Church and we believe we are receiving from them, grace and light. From where do they borrow the flame? Very possibly from the prayer of some devout and hidden soul whose inward shining is not apparent to human eyes. Some soul of unrecognised virtue, in her own estimation of small worth, indeed a dying flame!

"What mysteries we shall one day see unveiled! I have often mused that perhaps I owe all the graces with which I am laden to a little soul who I shall only know in heaven. It is God's will that here below on earth we distribute the heavenly treasures to one another by prayer. This is how He enriches us. This He does so that when they reach their everlasting home, they shall love one another with open hearts and with great affection far beyond that which pulses, even in the most perfect family circle here on earth.

"In heaven there can be no indifference to one another because all the saints owe so much to one another. No envious glances will be cast because the happiness of each one of the Blessed is the same happiness for everyone. With the Doctors of the Church we shall be Doctors; with the martyrs we shall be martyrs; with the virgins we shall be virgins. Just as members of one family are proud of each other, so without the least jealousy, we shall take immense pride in our heavenly brothers and sisters.

"When we see the great glory of the saints and realise that through the secret workings of Providence, we have been instrumental in their work, our joy in their bliss may be as intense and sweet as their own.

"Do you not grasp the possibility that the great Saints, knowing what they owe to us little souls, will love us with a love beyond compare? Friendship in Paradise will be delightful and full of surprises, of this I am certain. A shepherd boy will be a familiar friend of an Apostle or a great Doctor of the Church. A little child may be an intimate of a Patriarch. How I long to enter into the Kingdom of Love."

Our little sister teaches us:

Believe me; the smallest act of self-denial is worth more than the writing of pious books or beautiful poems. When we realise how incapable we are of doing anything of worth, we are devastated, then the best remedy by far is to offer to God the good works of others. Thus we know how great a gift is the Communion of Saints. Recall to mind now that ecstatic verse of our venerable father, Saint John of the Cross: 'Come back my dove, for you stir the breeze with the beat of your wings and bring cool refreshment to the wounded Hart upon the hill.'

The spouse is the wounded Hart. He is not comforted by the beauty of the hills but rather by the breeze from the downbeat of the wings of the dove, a refreshing caress which one single stroke of the wings can create.

The lowliest place on earth is the only place safe from envy. Here only here, is neither vanity nor spiritual pride. We recall, 'I know, Yahweh, no one's course is in his control, nor is it in anyone's power, as he goes on his way, to guide his own steps.' **(Jeremiah 10: 23)**. Often then our pride wells up and we long for the trappings that dazzle and delight. When this happens there is only one remedy. We must join and identify with the lowly and imperfect and know ourselves as very tiny souls who in every instant need the goodness of God to uphold us. He reaches out His hand to us in the very moment, when confirmed in our nothingness, He hears us cry out, 'I need only say, "I am slipping," for your faithful love, Yahweh, to support me' **(Psalms 94: 18)**. Should we attempt great things under the pretext of zeal, He leaves us. All we need to do is to humble ourselves and to bear humbly our imperfections.

Herein lies, for us, true holiness.

One day a novice told Saint Therese that she was more tired than her sisters because, beside her normal duties, she had worked hard on matters of which her sisters were unaware.

Saint Therese gave this counsel, "It would be a great joy for me to know you as a brave soldier, never complaining of the hardship, always concerned for your comrades, that their fatigue is always greater than your own. It is a general failing that we feel more fatigued because others know nothing of it.

"Blessed Margaret Mary revealed that when she had two whitlows, she only in fact suffered from one of them, the hidden one! Because the one she could not conceal was an object of compassion and her companions gave her great comfort because of it.

"It is a natural feeling that people should know of our aches and pains but when we pander to this need for sympathy, we are in fact cowards.

"When we are guilty of a fault, we must not blame a physical cause. We should not blame our faults on the weather or because we feel ill. We must acknowledge our faults without being discouraged by our lack of perfection.

"When the things happen they should not make us weak but should be cherished because when tried, we can demonstrate our strength in virtue. God did not permit our Mother to give me permission to write down my poems as soon as I composed them. I was afraid of asking leave of her lest I sin against the vow of poverty, so I had to wait for some free time in the evening at 8 o'clock. Then I often found it extremely difficult to recall what I had composed in the morning. These trifles are of course a form of martyrdom. We should bear them and not seek to avoid these little martyrdoms for we follow Jesus whose entire life here on earth was a daily agony."

> *My long slow martyrdom of fire still more and more consumed me. You are my joy, my one desire. Jesus, may I expire of Love for You!*
>
> *30th April 1896*

CHAPTER 11

SHARING GOD'S GIFTS

ONE DAY I WAS IN TEARS; SAINT Therese spoke to me telling me to shun the habit of letting my trifling concerns be seen by others. She reminded me that nothing made our community life more difficult than unevenness of temper.

I hastened to agree, for this I knew for myself. "From now on," I said, "I will keep my tears for God alone. I will confide my worries to the One who will understand and console me."

"Tears for God," she rejoined, "that will never do. Far less to Him than to His creatures should you display a mournful countenance. He comes to our cloisters in search of rest, to put aside the unceasing complaints of His friends in the world, who instead of appreciating the value of the Cross receive its burden more often with moans and tears rather than the smile of love. Clearly this is not disinterested love. We should seek to console Our Lord and not demand that He should ever console us. His Heart is so tender that if you weep He will always dry your tears but then He goes on His way saddened because you did not let Him rest tranquilly within you. Our Lord loves the glad heart of children as they greet Him with a smile. When you learn to set aside your troubles from Him or tell Him gaily that you are happy to suffer for His sake, then you will taste pure joy."

Then she added, "The face is the mirror of the soul and yours, just like a contented child, should ever be calm and serene. When you are alone, be cheerful for you are always in the sight of the Angels."

I was expecting her to congratulate me on what, in my view, was a heroic act of virtue, but instead she said to me:

"Now compare this small act of virtue with that which the Lord has of right to expect from you! Rather than seek praise, you should humble yourself for letting so many other opportunities of proving your love pass by unnoticed."

I was not at all happy with this rebuke as an answer. I determined to find out how she would react under trial, the occasion for which was not long in coming. Reverend Mother asked us to carry out some work, which bristled with difficulties, and on purpose, I made everything more difficult for our Novice Mistress. Not for one moment could I find any fault; regardless of the fatigue involved, she remained gracious and most amiable, ever eager to help anyone at her own expense. Eventually, I could stand it no longer and I told her all.

"How is it," I said, "that you are so patient? You are full of repose, always calm and full of joy."

"That was not always so with me," she replied, "only since I have stopped thinking about myself, do I live as happily as it is possible."

Meditate. *To know Him in suffering is to love Him for Himself. We love Him, Jesus the Christ, because He became flesh and lives with us. To live here with us, He shares our vulnerability to sin suffering And the eclipse of death. This is how we become brothers and sisters, daughters and sons of God. Our suffering is the reality of our redemption for He redeemed us through His suffering. It is not only a mystery but also a glorious truth that self-sacrifice is the flowering of hearts in eternity. The recycling of all material existence, to the highest existent being in constant repetition, Remind us as a sign of His care for us, out of Himself. Let us be perfect in our Love for Him, for in Him, The Holy One, shall we know perfection. Our failing to love Him with all our mind And all our heart is our weakness, Ever repaired in His suffering. For only in love of our Creator, can we come to perfection. In suffering for all, He opens the arms of reconciliation. Let us suffer here in joy that we shall know the gladness of the Resurrection.*

    Alleluia, Alleluia.

Saint Therese, guide us in our little way. Keep us small and glad to serve Him, Jesus our Saviour, Christ the King!

    Amen.

Our Mistress, the Saint, told us that during recreation, rather than at any other time, we should seek opportunities to practise virtue.

    "If you desire to profit, do not enter into recreation intent on enjoying yourself, instead go with the desire to entertain others and to practice self-denial. Then when you are telling one of your Sisters something which you believe is entertaining and she interrupts to tell you something different, show yourself to be attentive and interested, even though in reality, it is of none or little interest. Be careful then not to resume what you were saying. In this way you will depart from recreation with a great interior peace. You will find yourself endowed with fresh strength for the practice of virtue because you have not sought to please yourself but others. If only we could realise what we gain by self-denial in all things."

Certainly, Saint Therese, you achieved this for you always practised self-denial.

"Yes, I have forgotten myself and endeavoured not to seek myself in anything. When someone knocks at our door or when the bell rings for us, we must practise dying to ourselves and stop immediately whatever we are doing, even another stitch, and get up and answer." This, the Saint tells us is a great source of peace.

> **Meditate.** *When we put aside our own care and lift the veil on self-absorption, we come face to face with His Creation, which is very good. We are creatures made in His image and likeness but we do not have His gift of seeing ourselves as others see us. Joining others and being with them and perhaps serving them in this, we can see the face of God, His work and become real disciples. We are not required to be heroes but rather to be heroic in countless little ways. This is her little way of love, for in this way, she loved Our Lord and made His love known in the world.*

One novice followed her advice and, whenever the occasion arose, promptly answered every summons. During her illness, Saint Therese became aware of her sister's diligence in this matter and said this to her: "At the moment of your death, you will be very happy to have these good deeds to your credit. For you have achieved something more glorious than if you had succeeded in procuring the goodwill of government toward all the religious communities throughout France, as if you were a second Judith."

> **Meditate.** *The little way is filling the meadow with flowers that flourish and give joy to all – the balm and refreshment of His peace and compassion for all.*

Saint Therese was asked how she sanctified the daily bread of the Father.

"When we sit in the refectory for meals, our sole intention must be to perform a very ordinary action with most high reflections. I tell you that the sweetest aspirations of love often come to me at mealtimes. Sometimes I am overwhelmed by the realisation that Our Lord, were He seated in my place, would certainly take and eat from the very same dishes which are served to me.

"Is it not wonderful that it is most probable that during His lifetime He ate food like ours? It is certain that He must have eaten bread and fruit! Listen, here are my little rubrics. I imagine myself at Nazareth in the House of the Holy Family. If I am served with cold fish, wine or something savoury in taste, I offer it to Saint Joseph. Then to our Blessed Lady, I offer hot foods and ripe fruit and to the infant Jesus, I offer our feast day fare, especially rice and preserves. When, however, I am given a wretched meal, I say to myself with a smile, 'Today, my little one, it is all for you!'"

> **Meditate.** *The sharing of God's gifts is a spiritual actuality. We share in the reality of His gifts, our daily bread, in His ineffable goodness. This spiritual liveliness reminds us, enlightens us, to an awareness of our spiritual nature. We live bodily in all the material senses in the Spiritual world. When we come alive to our true spiritual selves then we slough off our drab earthliness and take on the glories of our Spiritual existence. We do not have two natures; we are just physical beings, persons in our spiritual natures. For we were made in his His image and likeness, and any image and likeness of God must be in essence spiritual because God is spirit. This tent of clay, which we inhabit, is not a metaphysical reality; it is a spiritual reality, the enclosure defined by its envelope of space.*

Thus the Saint teaches us that that which we consume as material sustenance, we can also give as the true expression of our sharing in the spiritual realities of His goodness.

Thus the Saint also kept from us mortals, in a delightful way, her mortifications. She did not wish to cast her pearls before swine. It was only the spiritual value of her mortifications she gave to God; this the world cannot recognise for we know pain and suffering only as loss and demeaning phenomena, we do not grasp them as the way from our mortal enclosure into His sheep pen, that is, through Him, who is the gateway, and in Him, His mystical body, His Church, this is the way in which we enter into the Kingdom.

One Fast Day, our Reverend Mother ordered for her some special food. She was found seasoning this food with wormwood because it was especially delightful to taste. On another occasion she drank her very unpleasant medicine most slowly. She was urged to drink it down in one go. "Oh no," she said, "I must take these small opportunities for penance since greater occasions are not available to me".

When we were talking in wonder of the mortifications of the Saints, she recalled the Word of God – "In my Father's house there are many rooms, if not I would have told you so! You see, if every soul called to perfection were obliged to perform such austerities in order to enter Heaven, He would have told us and we would willingly undertake them. However recall His words, 'there are many rooms in my Father's house'. There are some for heroic souls, for the Fathers of the Desert and for martyrs of penance, there must also be one for us little ones. In that place, if we love Him dearly with Our Father and the Spirit of love, is a place reserved for us."

> **Meditate.** *Perfection is not a contest setting one against another. It is an organic growth, a fruition of what we are, what we were created to be. Our incapacities, our fragility, our little strengths with the grace of God, we will come to Him as saints.*

The Saint recounts, "When I lived in the world, when I woke up, I would dread to think of all the pleasant and unpleasant things which might happen during the day. When I anticipated nothing but worries and unpleasantness, I used to get up with a heavy heart. Now it is the other way round. I think of the pain and suffering that awaits me and I arise feeling courageous and light-hearted in due proportion to the opportunities I have of proving my love for Our Lord and gaining – for I am a mother of souls – my children's life before God. Then I kiss my crucifix, laying it gently on my pillow. I leave it there while I dress, saying, 'My Jesus, you toiled and wept enough during your thirty-three miserable years here on earth. Rest today, for it is my turn to fight and suffer.'"

One washing day, I was sauntering along on my way to the laundry, looking at the flowers. Saint Therese passed me and remarked softly, "Is that the way people walk when they have children and have to work to feed them? Do you know which are my Sundays and Holy days? They are the days on which God tries me most."

I was upset at my lack of courage and our Saint said to me, "You are complaining of a weakness which ought to be your greatest happiness. If you fight only when you feel ready for the fray, what merit would you be worthy of? What does it matter if you have no courage, provided you behave as if you were truly brave? If you feel too tired to pick up a bit of thread, yet you do so for the love of Jesus, you gain more merit than you would for a much nobler action carried through on an impulse of fervour. Instead of feeling sorry for yourself, be glad that Our Lord is made known to you. Your own weakness is presenting you with the opportunity of saving a great number of souls."

A sister asked the Saint whether Our Lord was displeased at her many failings. "Have no fear," she said. "He whom you have chosen as your spouse has every perfection but I tremble to say it, He is blind and so ignorant of arithmetic that He can't even add up! The two defects would be deplorable if He were an earthly bridegroom, yet in this He is infinitely more loveable. You see, if He saw each and every one of our sins and was so quick with figures as to reckon their number in an instant, He would return us at once to nothingness, but you see His love for us renders Him blind and indifferent to the number of our transgressions. If the greatest sinner from earth should repent at the moment of death and breathe his last breath as an act of love, then none of the many graces refused nor the many sins committed would stand against him. Our Lord would see nothing and count nothing except the sinner's last prayer, then without delay, He would take him into the arms of His mercy.

"To render Him blind and incapable of reckoning our sins, we must come to Him through His Heart – in this way He is defenceless."

A sister once had grieved her and in sorrow went to ask her pardon. The Saint proclaimed, "Never have I understood the love with which Jesus receives us when we seek His forgiveness with such clarity! If I, His poor little creature, feel such utter tenderness that you have come back to me, what must pass through Our Lord's heart when we return to Him? Much quicker than I have done, will He blot out our sins from His memory. He will love us more tenderly than before we fell."

> **Meditate.** *Adam's disobedience fanned the flames of God's love and kindled the fire of His compassion to so great a degree that He sent us His only son to die for us and save all.*
>
> **Alleluia, Alleluia.**

*Let us look upon the Lord with love for He is love
and, in love, we behold creation through His eyes. Let
our faith endure forever and our hope shine out from
us like the bridal gown. For her salvation is in His
embrace and her redemption in the clasp of her arms
about His neck – **Blessed be God forever!***

Another recollection reveals to us how a sister had an intense
dread of the judgement of God. Nothing that the Saint said
could remove that terror. One day the afflicted one put to her
the following objection: "We are taught that, in the sight of
God, even the angels are not pure. How can I then be anything
other than full of fear?"

She replied, "There is only one way of compelling God not
to judge us. We must go before Him empty-handed."

"How can I do that?"

"Simply this, lay nothing by, use your treasures as fast
as you gain them. If I live to be eighty, I shall always be
poor because I cannot save; all my creditable gain is spent
immediately upon the ransom of souls. If I waited for the hour
of death to tender my trifling coin, Our Lord would find in
them some base metal and then they would have to be refined
in Purgatory. It has been said even of great Saints, when they
come before the divine tribunal their hands full with merit,
that even then they had to go to that place of expiation, because
in God's eyes all our justice is unclean."

I replied, "As God does not judge our good deeds, surely
will He judge our bad ones?"

"Don't say that! Our Lord is justice itself, and as He will
not judge our good deeds, neither will He judge our bad ones!
It seems clear to me that for victims of love there will be no

judgement. God will rather hasten to reward with eternal delights His own love which he will gaze upon in their hearts."

"To enjoy such a privilege would it suffice to say the act of contrition which you have composed?"

"Oh no, words will not do. To be a true victim of love, we must surrender ourselves completely. Love will consume us only in the measure of our self-surrender."

> **Meditate.** *We must let go and be drawn into the flames of His Sacred Heart. Thus we will become perfect, as He is perfect. In this command He offers Himself completely to all who come before Him and offer themselves. For our perfection is the will of His Father the Creator that all will be handed back, all in all.*

I was grieving most bitterly after committing a grave sin. "Take your crucifix," she said, "and kiss it." I kissed the feet.

"Is that how a child kisses its Father? Throw your arms around His neck and kiss His face." When I had done this, she said, "That is not sufficient, for He must respond to your caress." I had to press the crucifix to both cheeks. She then said, "Now all is forgiven."

One day the Saint was told that if a sister was going to be rebuked, she could accept this much better when it was deserved than when she was unjustly reproached. The Saint said, "I prefer to be rebuked unjustly, for then I have nothing to confess and I can offer this little injustice to God. Then in humility, I recall how often I have deserved such a reproach. The better you grow in goodness, then victory over yourself becomes less of a battle because you see more clearly the way of Christ. Then your soul on the wings of love will soar above worldly creation. For me, I am utterly indifferent to all accusations because I have learnt the shallowness of all human judgement. We cannot benefit from defending ourselves when misunderstood and wrongly convicted. Leave matters as they are, say nothing. It is good to be judged rightly or wrongly.

"It is written in the Gospel that Mary gave no excuse when her sister charged her with idleness when she sat at Our Lord's feet. She did not say in answer, 'Martha, if you could share my happiness hearing these words, you too would leave your work and join me here.' No she kept silent, blessed silence which brings such peace to our souls."

> **Meditate.** *Silence lets the Heart speak and the ear listen to the voice of God. Silence is the tune of obedience waiting only for His command.*

At a moment of struggle and temptation for one of her sisters, the Saint wrote and sent this note:

The just man will correct me in mercy and reprove me, but never let the oil of the sinner perfume my head. All my sisters are pleasing to God, only the just can correct me. It is less bitter to be accused by the sinner than by the just, but in compassion for sinners and to obtain their conversion, I beg thee, O my God, to allow that I am roundly condemned by these just souls who surround me. I ask also that the oil of praise, so welcome to our inclinations, may not perfume my head, that is my mind, by making me believe that I am virtuous when all I have done is a few trifling good deeds.

Jesus, your name is an oil poured out! And it is in this divine perfume that I desire to hide myself from this world. It is not in the spirit of the game to argue with a sister even when she is in the wrong because we are not answerable for her conduct. We are not Justices of the Peace, but Angels of Peace.

> **Meditate.** *We face judgement alone. The charge will be that echoing enquiry of God in the Garden. It will say, "What have you done?" Nothing else will matter and our judgements will cause us great concern! Listen with care my brothers and sisters!*

"You worry and care too much about your work," she often said to us. "You worry about the future as if it were in your hands. You are concerned at this time about what is happening in other convents of the Carmelite order and worry whether the nuns there are diligent or otherwise. Does their work prevent you from your prayers and meditations? Well, in the same way, detach yourselves from your own personal labours; attend to them most diligently but with perfect freedom of heart. It is written that the Israelites, whilst building the walls of Jerusalem, worked with one hand and held a sword with the other. This is a sign for our conduct, that we should avoid being totally absorbed in our work."

> **Pray**. *Let our work, Lord Jesus, fill your heart with joy. Let us, in obedience, come to you. May we mount Calvary at your side and by the manger pray. Jesus, our joy, reach out to us, your delight in being here on earth. God is with us in our work. Let us rest upon His breast.*
> *Amen, Amen.*

CHAPTER 12

THE CHRISTMAS LETTER

"ONE SUNDAY," THE SAINT SAID, "I WENT to the chestnut avenue, my heart full of gladness. It was springtime and I wanted to enjoy the beauties of nature. I was bitterly disappointed, our dear chestnuts had been heavily pruned, the branches, covered with buds, lay on the floor. I reflected on this havoc, that it would be three years before the damage could be repaired. My heart was very sore. My grief did not last; I recalled that if I were in another convent, I would know nothing of the chestnut trees of the Carmel of Lisieux, even if they cut them down to the root. I will not fret over things that pass. God shall be my all; I will take my walks in the wooded groves of His love whereon none would dare lay hands."

> **Meditate.** *His gifts are there before us in Creation, the work of His Word. There, beauty is a pledge of His care and compassion for all His creatures.*

A novice asked some sisters to help her shake out some blankets. They were old and worn and the novice was strident in her demands that the blankets must be treated with care. The Saint said to the impatient novice, "Would you be so demanding of others if it was not your duty to mend these blankets? There should be no thought of self-interest in this matter; if you must draw attention to this matter, do it in an impersonal way. In all our actions we must avoid self-serving."

One of our sisters was very tired. I said to our mistress, "It is hard for me to see people suffering, especially those who are holy."

She immediately said, "I don't feel like that. Saints who suffer do not provoke my pity. I know they have the strength to bear their sufferings and that in this, they give great glory to God. However, I have great compassion for those who are not saints and who do not know how to gain merit from suffering. My pity is awakened and I would strain every nerve to help them and bring them comfort.

"If I were to live for a long time, I would delight in being given the office of Infirmarian. I would never ask for it, but if it were imposed in obedience, I should be 'most highly favoured'. I would place all my heart into this work, bearing in mind Our Lord's words 'I was sick and you visited me'. **(Matthew 25:36)**

"The infirmary bell should be heavenly music for us and we should linger as we pass the open windows so that the sick can call for us more easily. Consider yourself as a little slave of whom everyone, everyone has the right to command. If you could see the Angels who watch our struggles from the heights of heaven, you would understand that they are waiting for the end of combat so that they can crown you and cover you with flowers. You are aware that we aspire to the rank of 'little martyrs', remember we must win our palms. God does not deride these hidden struggles; they are richer in merit for they go unseen; we must however, win our palms.

"These hidden struggles within ourselves are not unseen before God and they are rich in merit because they are not done upon the stage of this world. The patient man is more worthy than the brave and valiant. He who has command of himself is more worthy than he who leads the storm troopers.

"Through our little acts of charity, practised unseen, we obtain the conversion of the heathen, help missionaries in their need for alms. This is how we build both spiritual and material dwellings for our Eucharistic God."

I thought that Mother Prioress showed more confidence and affection to another sister than she had for me. Expecting some sympathy, I mentioned this to my Novice Mistress. I was surprised when she asked, "Do you think that you love our Mother very much?"

"Certainly," I said, "that's why I feel hurt when she prefers others to me."

"Well now, let me show you how mistaken you are. You see it is not our Mother you love, but rather yourself! When we truly love others, then we are delighted in their happiness; in fact, we make every sacrifice to make them happy. Therefore, if your affection was true and without self-interest, loving our Mother for her own sake, you would be glad to see her happy even at your own expense. Now if she is happier talking to your sister, you ought not to feel hurt at this neglect, but instead be happy in her happiness."

> **Meditate.** *When the one whom you love is happy, surely you are content, at peace, rejoicing that the one you love is full of joy! Joy in the delight of others.*

> *When we say, or pray, 'look at me, come to me, speak*
> *to me' or even 'love me', we must always ask 'is this*
> *self-love or love given freely and accepted with humble*
> *amazement?' We are beloved of the Father, His sons*
> *and daughters and our relationship as daughters and*
> *sons is founded in love, His love for us. We are beloved*
> *of God. It is His love which shines in our eyes when*
> *we love one another.*

A sister told her that she was upset by many distractions when she was praying. "I also have many distractions and this is how I try to benefit from these interruptions. As soon as I am distracted, I pray for those who are distracting me and breaking my concentration. In this way, they reap the benefits of my distractions. I accept all these things, even the wildest fancies that cross my mind, for the love of God." Another sister recalled that she was irritable and grumbling in regret that she had given away a pin that she had found most useful! The Saint remarked gently, "How rich you are in your suffering, you will never be happy!"

The grotto of the Holy Child was in her charge and, knowing that one of our Mothers greatly disliked perfumes, she never put sweet-smelling flowers there, not even a tiny violet. This was a great sorrow for she loved the wild perfumes of God's Creation. One day, as she was placing a beautiful artificial rose at the foot of the statue, the Mother who disliked perfume, called her sternly. Anticipating that she would be ordered to remove the rose, and in order to spare her Mother any embarrassment, she took the flower with her to the good nun saying, "Look, Mother, how well nature is imitated these days, you would be forgiven if you thought that it had been just freshly cut from the bush."

> **Meditate.** *Perfume is a mark of holiness, it tells passers-by to come and taste the sweetness of His beauty given to us. The invitation is free without constraint. This is how we should pray, like perfumed flowers, witnesses to passers-by of His love, His perfection. He is the apple of our eye. Taste and know how sweet is the Lord.*
>
> *BWF*

"There are moments," she taught us, "when we are so miserable within ourselves that the only relief and right thing to do is to get away from ourselves. At these times, we are not obliged by the love of God to remain at home in our hearts. He instead gives us this opportunity, when our own company becomes unbearable, that we may escape and grow in another place. Now the only way to escape from ourselves is in the service of others; these charitable works we can do on our way to visit Jesus and Mary."

> **Meditate.** *The Holy Family is our family and we should visit Jesus and Mary and call to see St Joseph. They are only down the road, not far away. Maybe we should call upon them every day.*
> **Alleluia, Alleluia.**

The Saint tells us: "When I recall to mind the Holy Family, it is their ordinary simplicity in their family home life which lifts my spirits and fills me with tranquil repose. Our Lady and Saint Joseph were well aware that Jesus was God, yet the grasp of these great wonders was hidden from them and beyond their ken. Like us in this, they lived by faith. We have listened to the Word of God, 'But they did not understand what he meant', and after Simeon had quoted Isaiah of Him in the Nunc Dimittis, 'the child's mother and father were wondering at the things that were spoken of Him'. They were surprised and astonished at these revelations, for the word 'wondering' implies an attempt to understand that which is not fully grasped and understood."

> **Meditate.** *At home in Nazareth, a simple life was led with Jesus, true man and true God, the Son at rest. The only Son of God cared for and loved by human parents. Joseph and Mary lived by faith, guiding the Wonderful Counsellor in their midst. To have such tender care for God's only Son, this is our Christian destiny, to know His presence here in the Ark of His love, His Church. Revealed in faith is the Word made flesh and the Cross the eternal sign of suffering, love raising us up in the Resurrection. Joseph and Mary, in obedience to a tyrant's law, set out from Nazareth to Bethlehem, on a journey with Jesus, which led to Gethsemane and the Golden Gate to Calvary and beyond. The home of God, here in our midst, is the Little Way of Love.*
>   *Amen.*

"There is a verse in the Divine Office which I say each day with some temerity and small reluctance. 'I incline my heart in obedience to your statutes, their reward is eternal life.' **(Psalms 118: 112)** I hasten to add, in my heart, 'My Jesus, you know that I do not serve you for the sake of reward, but only out of love and a desire to win you souls.'

"Only in heaven shall we grasp the clear transparent truth. Here on earth, even with the aid of Holy Scripture, we see only dimly. It distresses me to see the differences with which we guild it in translation. Had I been a cleric, I would have learnt Aramaic Hebrew so that I could read the Word of God as He gave it to us in human speech."

It is recalled of our sister, the Saint: "She often told me of a well-known toy with which she often played as a child. This was the kaleidoscope, shaped like a small telescope, through which, as it is made to revolve, one can see an endless variety of pretty coloured patterns and figures."

"This toy," she said, "excited my imagination. For a long time I wondered what could produce such a charming phenomenon. One day, on very careful examination, I found that it consisted of tiny pieces of coloured paper and cloth scattered inside. On closer examination, I found three mirrors juxtaposed inside the tube and the problem was resolved. It became for me the illustration of a great and complex truth."

The Saint teaches us: "As long as our deeds, even the most trivial actions, remain within love's kaleidoscope, the Blessed Trinity, figured by the three mirrors, imparts to them a wonderful brightness and beauty interlocked, yet ever-changing, in an eternal set of figures and patterns. The eyepiece is Jesus Christ Himself, and He, looking from outside through Himself into the kaleidoscope of the Holy Trinity, finds all our works perfect. Should we ever leave that ineffable abode of love (His mystical Body, His Church), He would see nothing but the worthless chaff of worthless deeds."

Meditate. *All we have to offer the Prince of Peace, Wonderful Counsellor, Mighty God, Eternal Father, are pieces of cloth and shards of coloured glass. In the prism of immortal love, three in One, this base, human, tattered remnant is now incarnate in His heart. This transformation is the perfect illustration of His love, Father, Son and Holy Spirit, in a manger born. The kaleidoscope of perfect love, mirrored in Our Saviour's birth. Perfect us as we come to Him, born from above, whence comes God's only Son. Let us cleave to Him, His Church, for He is there, on the Altar of Salvation. In Him, there is perfection, He is the offering. In Him is our perfection, our transformation. From beads and rags to the Beatific Vision, let us remain in Him, then we are His Church, the tattered remnant flying at the mast. In Him, through Him, with Him, He perfects our world. Let us never leave His ineffable abode of love. We are His Holy Family when we go home, at home, with Joseph and Mary, sustained in simple faith and Love.*

Alleluia, Alleluia.

I spoke to her of the strange power, produced by what some call a magnetic force, on persons who surrender their will to a hypnotiser. It interested her a great deal, and next day, she said to me, "Your conversation of yesterday did me a great deal of good. I now have a great longing to be hypnotised by Our Lord! It was my waking thought and I was delighted and ecstatic to surrender to Him my will. I want Him now to take possession of my faculties in such a way that my acts are no longer mine, or even human acts but divine acts, inspired and guided by the Spirit of Love."

Just before my profession, I received through the intercession of my saintly Novice Mistress, a very special grace. We had been washing all through the day and I was fatigued and under emotional stress because I was in turmoil with great and intense spiritual worries. This night, before meditation, I approached her to unburden my soul. She however, avoided any intimate talk and then cut me short, remarking, "That is the bell for meditation, I have not time to comfort you and I can see no words of mine will suffice. For the present," she said, "God wishes that you suffer alone." I followed her to meditation crestfallen and dismayed – for the first time I doubted my vocation! It came to me that I would never be able to be a Carmelite; the life was too hard to bear!

I knelt in meditation, lost in this interior struggle, when in an instant, without having asked or desired peace, there came an extraordinary change in my whole being. I was lost to myself. My vocation was now to me both beautiful and most loveable. I comprehended without any effort the sublime sweetness and incomparable value of suffering. All the fatigue and privations of our religious life became infinitely preferable to the pleasures of the world and I arose from my meditation absolutely transformed.

During the next day, I informed our Novice Mistress what had happened in meditation. She was visibly moved and I asked her the reason. She said very clearly, "God is good. You inspired in me before meditation, profound compassion and pity, so that I prayed for you incessantly throughout our meditations. I beseeched Our Lord to bring you peace and to comfort you; to change your doubts to joy and reveal to you the inestimable value of suffering. He has heard my prayers."

> **Meditate.** *Faith has moved mountains and prayers have delivered the poor to life eternal. To pray is to be invited to the Banquet of the Lord. To be summoned to His presence and feel the hand of God. Prayer removes us from the cage of this world and transports us to heaven. For He is in heaven and the escalator of sincere prayer transports us, bathed in love, to stand before Him in peaceful contemplation. Thus when we ask His will to change things into goodness, will we ever be indulged and given that great reward of perfect peace.*

A novice tells us this astonishing story of an event which will live forever in the heart of mankind and in God. I was childlike in my ways and the Holy Child Jesus inspired me with the thought of playing with Him; this would help me to practise virtue and so I chose a special game of ninepins. First of all I imagined the ninepins in all shapes and sizes and colours so that they represented those souls I desired to touch with His love. My love for the Holy Child Jesus then became the ball.

In December 1896, the novices received from benefactors, for the benefit of foreign missions, various small presents for the Christmas tree. At the bottom of the box containing these trinkets was a top, which was a novelty in a Carmelite convent. My companions looked at the top and said, "What an ugly, useless thing! Whatever do you use it for?" I took it from them because I recognised it and was familiar with the game. "It's great fun," I told them, "it will spin and spin all day without stopping if whipped properly." Then I showed them how to do it, to their astonishment. Our saintly Mistress watched all this in silence. On Christmas night, after midnight Mass, I found in our cell the famous top and a letter addressed as follows:

To my beloved little spouse, player of ninepins on the mountain of Carmel, Christmas Night 1896.

My beloved little spouse,

I am well pleased with you; all the year round you have given me joyful pleasure with your game of ninepins. I was so overjoyed that the whole court of Angels was delighted and charmed. They were so taken with your game that several little cherubs asked why I did not make them children. Some others enquired about the pleasure in the melody of their instruments and which pleased me most, their playing or the joyful celebrations when a ninepin fell flat at the touch of your love ball. I told them that they must not regret that they are not children like you because, one day, they would play with you in the meadows of heaven. I told them that your smiles were more precious to me than their melodies because these smiles were bought by suffering and selflessness.

Now my cherished spouse, I am going to ask you for something. I know you will not refuse because you love me so much. Let us change the game; ninepins are a great joy but now I would like you to play at spinning the top. If you agree, you will be the 'top'. I gave you one as a model.

It is ugly and insignificant to all who do not know how to play the game. A little child would leap and shout for joy when she saw it. "What fun", she would say, "I will make it spin all day without stopping." Now, although you too are not attractive, I, the Infant Jesus, love you and I urge you to keep on spinning to delight and amuse me. It is true that a top needs a whip to keep it spinning, so let your sisters supply the whip of authority and obedience and you will be most grateful to them as you turn ever faster.

When I have had a surfeit of joyous amusement, then I shall call you to join me here and our games will be full of perfect delight. Thy little brother, Jesus.

Meditate.

This letter is the greatest ever written, for it was inspired and written from on high. It teaches us that heaven is very close and that the innocence of perfection makes us infants again in the arms of Our Father. It teaches us to make use, full use, of Jesus' love for us. He is a ball of infinite love, our ball, our focus, the movement of which we must follow and delight in. No one possesses this ball of love yet we can all use and conquer with it. We must use the ball of love to win Him souls. Let us pray through Him and in Him and with Him and strike those ninepins so that they fall for Him and serve Him.

Let us look forward to those meadows in heaven where we shall play with the Cherubs and listen to their melodies as we delight in the perfection of our perfection, moulded in His love. To be moulded and

172

transformed in love like Him, we must suffer the agonies of this world as it is transformed into the perfection of the world of heaven.

Let us spin in obedience, as the world spins in conformity with the laws of His creation. As we spin in obedience, we are drawn ever closer to Him, Our Saviour, Our Maker, Our Friend.

Pray for us, Saint Therese, here on the battlefield of salvation. May your prayers bowl us over and your laughter raise us to heaven.

Amen, Amen.

CHAPTER 13

LIVING IN FAITH

A sister tells us: "I had the habit of crying over little things and this troubled our Mistress. One day an ingenious resolution for my sensitivity came to her. She took a mussel shell in which she mixed paint from the painting table, then holding my hands to stop me from resisting her, she gathered up my tears in the shell. Soon, tears turned to laughter. "Now I permit you to cry as much as you like, always provided that it is into this shell!"

A week before her death, I cried throughout the evening at the thought of her approaching demise. She realised this when I saw her and said to me, "You have been crying, was it into the shell?"

I told her the truth and she was troubled. "I am about to die and I will only rest if you promise faithfully to follow my advice! I reckon this to be most important for your good and the good of your soul."

I promised but asked leave, as a favour, that I should be allowed to cry at her death. "Why cry at my death?" she said; "those tears will be misplaced. You will be sorrowing for my happiness. Yet I have pity on your weakness, so for the first few days you may cry, then you must take up the shell."

It has been very difficult sometimes, but I have been faithful. I keep the shell on me and when I am overcome with the urge to cry, I take hold of the pitiful thing. However urgent the tears, the trouble of passing it from one eye to the other completely distracts me and I am then entirely cured by this incongruous remedy.

Owing to a fault of mine by which I had caused her much pain, of which I was deeply repentant, I resolved to deprive myself of Holy Communion. I wrote her a note explaining my resolution; this was her reply:

"Little Flower most dear to Jesus, by this humiliation your roots are sustained by the soil of this earth. You must now open wide your petals and lift high your head so that the manna of the Angels may, like divine dew, come down to strengthen you and supply your wants. Goodnight, poor little flower! Ask Jesus that all of the prayers offered for my cure may serve to increase the fire which ought to consume me."

> **Meditate.** *Little Therese you are with us, teach us how to play and smile. May your vision, the sight of Our Lady in Heaven, enlighten us and give us joy. For in these gifts we are most Blessed and our suffering is a pathway among the flowers.*

"At the time of offertory, just before Communion, it is as if my soul was like unto a child of three or four whose hair is ruffled and whose clothes have been rumpled while at play. This is the image I have. Often I have been struggling to save souls, but our Blessed Lady comes promptly to my rescue. She takes off my dishevelled pinafore, arranges my hair, adorning it with a pretty ribbon or a flower. Then I am presentable and able to take my seat at the Banquet of Angels without having to blush."

> **Meditate.** *When we take our seat with the Angels at the table of His Body and Blood, Saint Therese be with us there so that seeing you, we will remember.*
>
> *Ask Our Lady for the grace of preparation so that we shall always be worthy to taste and know the sweetness of Our Lord Jesus. May we ever be ready to walk with Him, ready to suffer for Him and wait on Him.*
>
> *He has saved us from our sins and enfolds us in the Spirit of Love – His ever-open arms on the Cross. Through His death may we come into Paradise as we enter through His death.*
>
> *Alleluia.*

In the infirmary, we scarcely waited for the end of her thanksgiving before we sought her counsel and advice. At first, this counsel caused her consternation and she rebuked us gently, then she would smile and was heard to say, "I must not seek rest and repose any more than Our Lord. When He withdrew into the hills after preaching, the crowds followed Him and disturbed His solitude. Come then, to me as much as you wish, I must go sword in hand, 'the sword of the Spirit', that is, the Word of God."

> **(Ephesians 6: 14–17)** *So stand your ground with truth a belt around your waist, with uprightness as a breastplate and as footwear, 'the eagerness to spread*

the Gospel of Peace' and always carrying the shield of faith so that you can use it to douse the burning arrows of the evil one! Then you must take Salvation as your helmet and the sword of the Spirit, that is, the Word of God.

Meditate. *From her bed of sickness and suffering, Little Therese was a true shepherd. 'As He stepped ashore He saw a large crowd and He was full of compassion for them because they were like sheep without a shepherd'.* **(Mark 6: 34)**

Saint Therese, bring us home, guide us to Him, Our Saviour Jesus the Christ. He is the true shepherd. He is the entrance into the sheepfold and He is the sheepfold, His mystical body. He is the Church, the Sacred Heart of His Church, Sacrifice, Victim, Offering and Redeemer.

We asked with great eagerness, "Tell us how we can profit from our spiritual instruction."

"I opened to my beloved
but he had turned his back and gone
My soul failed at his flight
I sought him but I did not find Him
I called to Him but he did not answer
The watchmen came upon me
as they made their rounds in the city
They beat me they wounded me

They took away my cloak
they who guard the ramparts."
(The Fourth poem of the Bride.
Verses 6 and seven)

"When you go for spiritual guidance, go with great simplicity. Do not raise up your hopes or rely on help, human aid which might fail you at any time, for then you would have to, like the Beloved Spouse in the Canticle, 'The watchmen took my cloak and beat me. When I escaped from them, I found Him whom my soul loves.'

"If you ask with profound humility and detachment about your Beloved, then the watchmen will tell you how to find Him. Very often you will find Jesus only when you have given up all creatures. I often repeat this verse of the Spiritual Canticle of St John of the Cross.

> "*Messengers, please, no more dialogue. You know not*
> *how to tell me what my spirit longs to know. For they*
> *may read His words and forever tell a thousand more*
> *yet make all my wounds to bleed a little deeper than*
> *before. Then I know nothing and my Spirit grieves*
> *with such vague stammerings I am bereaved.*

"It would not trouble me, supposing the impossible, if God Himself were not aware of my actions. I love Him so much that I would be happy to give Him joy without His knowing who gave it. You see when He knows, then He is obliged to reciprocate. I do not like to trouble Him.

"Had I been rich I would never have let anyone go hungry.

This is why, in my spiritual life, I give all merit away. You see, there are many souls on the brink of Hell and as soon as I earn anything, it is shared among sinners. The time has never come when I could say, 'Now I am going to work for myself.''

"Many people fear the worst in everything. I am not like this. I always see the best in everything, then even if it is my lot to suffer without a ray of comfort, then I will make that my joy."

> **Meditate.** *Christ, true God and true man suffered. He emptied Himself of His Glory and became man, living here among death and sin. Thus God's only Son redeemed us in our freedom. All is changed now; death is the only way to Redemption. When we suffer and die in Him, then we shall be resurrected to Salvation. His Beloved, in Him*
>   *Alleluia.*

"Whatever has come from God's hand has always pleased me, even when those gifts seemed less beautiful than those He gave to others. As a little girl staying with my Aunt, I read a story in which a schoolmistress was highly praised for her tact in settling disputes without hurting anyone. She would say to one party, 'You are quite right', then to the other party, 'You are not in the wrong'. As I read this I rejected its theme. I could not behave like this, one must always tell the truth. I will always tell the truth, even when it is most unpleasant for me. It would be less trouble when a novice comes with a grievance to blame those who are absent. Less trouble yet I always say exactly what I mean. If I am disliked that cannot be helped. The novices must not come to me if they do not want to be told the truth."

Meditate. *Little Therese, come to me and tell me the truth.*

"Any rebuke [to a novice] must bear a cost and be free from all emotion if it is to bear fruit. Kindness must not decline into weakness. When there is good reason to find fault, we must not worry over having given pain. It does more harm than good to seek out a delinquent for the purpose of consoling her. Left to her own devices she must seek consolation from God. Then she is forced to recall her faults and humble herself before Him. If this is not done then she will come to expect to be consoled when she deserves to be corrected. Then she will be acting like a small spoilt child who stamps and screams, knowing that, by this behaviour, her mother will come and dry her tears."

"'Let the sword of the Spirit which is the Word of God, be ever in your mouth and in your hearts' **(Ephesians 6: 17)**. If a novice is difficult and disagreeable, we must not lose heart and stop trying to help her reform. We must not pass over problems for the sake of our own comfort. The war must go on even when there is small hope of victory. We must wield the sword of the Spirit and help her correct her faults. Success is not the goal; we must continue the struggle for souls. We must never say, 'I shall not succeed with that person, she does not understand, I give up with her.' That is to act like a coward and deserter. We must do our duty to the very end.

"Do you know that if any of my friends in trouble were not consoled when they came to see me, I would leave the parlour quite heartbroken. Our Lord made me understand that I was quite incapable of bringing comfort to all. Now I no longer grieve when my visitors go away still downcast. I confide to

God the sufferings of those most dear to me and I am sure that He hears my prayers. At their next visit, I learn that I was not mistaken. I, therefore, no longer worry if I have given pain involuntarily. I quite simply ask Our Lord to make amends."

> **Meditate.** *Let us ask Jesus to help us in our weakness. When we fail others, may He put right our inadequacies. We, in obedience and out of His loving command, love our neighbours with our little love. We ask for His love to flow into the breach, healing and comforting all those whom we fail. In our weakness there is His mighty arm that wields the sword of the Spirit which is the word of God. The Word was made flesh and dwells among us. Jesus, in the weakness of accepting death, you are triumphant. We offer to you our weakness, the little way of love, that you will comfort those in whom we fail to shine your light. Light of the world, may the shadows we cast pass away in the littleness of our Love for God. For you perfect our littleness so that it becomes an acceptable offering. Let us become like tiny mustard seeds dying with you, resting in you, rising through you, a haven for many.*
>
> ***Amen, Amen!***

"What do you say of all the graces that have been given to you?" I reflect, "the Spirit of God breathes where He wills."

This, the Saint teaches of Faith:

"Mother," she said on one occasion, "were I unfaithful or if I committed the slightest infidelity, I know my soul would be filled with anguish and I would be unable to welcome death." When the Prioress showed alarm and concern that she should speak like this, she said, "I am speaking of infidelity in the matter of pride. For example, if I were to say, 'I have acquired this virtue and I can practise it'. Or again, 'My God, thou knowest I love thee too much to dwell on one single thought against faith', I should immediately be overcome by the most overwhelming temptations that I would give way to them. To prevent this misfortune, I say humbly from the heart, 'My God, I plead with you, don't let me be unfaithful!'"

> **Meditate.** *Faith is a gift from God. It does not come to us by the merit of intellect or understanding. Faith blinds us that we may come to see the Glory of God in the tiny infant helpless in the Incarnation.*
> **Alleluia**.

"I understand clearly how Peter fell. He placed too much reliance on his ardent loving nature instead of leaning on God. He only had to say, 'Lord, give me strength to follow you unto death!' and the grace would have been granted. 'How is this,' they ask Mother, 'that our Lord, aware of what was to happen, did not say to save him, "Ask of me for the courage to be faithful"?' I believe that His purpose was a twofold lesson for us:

"First: He taught His Apostle this, that even in His presence, which is available to us through the inspiration of grace, can we remain steadfast in His love, in sole reliance on Him.

"Second: Having made the choice of Peter to lead His Church, in which there are many sinners, He wanted Peter to know of Himself what little man can do without God's help. That explains Jesus saying to him before his failure: And the Lord said, 'Simon, Simon, look, Satan has got his wish to sift you all like wheat. But I have prayed for you, Simon, that your faith may not fail'. **(Luke 22: 31–32)**

"Once you have recovered, you in your turn must strengthen your brothers. In other words, tell them the story of your sin and show them, by your own experience, how necessary it is for salvation to rely solely on me!"

Watching her in so much pain, I said often to her, "Life is so dreary." She would always respond immediately, "Life is not dreary; it is most gay and full of joy! If you were to say instead 'exile is dreary' then I would understand. We are mistaken to understand life as having an end. The word should only be used in relation to the joys of heaven, joys that never fade and never end. Then, understanding the true meaning of life, it is never sad but gay and full of joy."

In the summary of her call to Sainthood, it is recorded that she said on one occasion, "I am always gay and content, even when I suffer. It is written of some Saints that even when they relaxed and rested they were austere and grave. This does not attract me; I prefer the example of Theophane Venard – he was always light-hearted and full of fun."

This extraordinary charity made her bright and cheerful. When she could not go to recreation, the nuns were disappointed. They said to each other, "There will be less laughter and jollity today, Sister Therese is not with us."

She had a wonderful sense of humour. For sometime she had been feeling much better and we teased her, "We are not sure what disease you will die of."

She said, "I shall die of death! Didn't God say to Adam, 'You are doomed to die'?"

She taught us: "Will then, death come to fetch you? No, not death, but Almighty God. Death should not be depicted as a ghastly phantom or terrible spectre. The Catechism teaches that death is the separation of soul from body, nothing more. Well then, I do not fear a separation that will unite me forever to God! Will then, the Divine Purloiner, they asked, come soon to pluck His little bunch of grapes? I see Him far off and I cry out, 'this way, this way!' rather than 'stop thief!'"

We asked her what name should we pray to her in heaven. She said most humbly, "Call to me, 'Little Therese'."

> **Meditate.** *Little Therese, we pray to you in heaven. Come down as you said you would and work with us on the battlefield of salvation. Come amongst us and guide us in the little way of love. We will greet you with laughter and smiles and throw petals of love to Him, Our Saviour. We are little, like you, and go in love. Empty-handed, teach us to rejoice in death for we long to be with you in Heaven. With you then, we shall see the kaleidoscope of the Beatific Vision.*
> **Alleluia.**

She was told by a sister that 'beautiful angels, all robed in white' would bear her soul up to heaven. "That is a fanciful understanding. It does not help me, my soul can only feed on the truth. You see, God and His angels are pure spirits. We cannot behold them as they are. That is why I have never asked for supernatural favours. I will wait for the Eternal Beatific Vision.

"I do not ask God for any consolations such as a beautiful dream at my death. As you wish to resemble me, remember what I have written, 'Fear not, O Lord, that I shall wake thee, I shall wait in peace on the heavenly beach.'

"It is a great joy to serve God in the dark night in the midst of trial. Recall at the end, we only have this life in which we can live in faith."

> **Meditate.** *To live in faith is to abandon yourself to love. We do not know our Love for him, until we abide in Him.*

"I am very happy at the thought of going to heaven, but when I reflect on these words of Our Lord: 'I will come soon and my reward is with me, I will render to everyone according to their deeds.' **(Revelation 22: 12)** He will find in my case a cause of concern; I have no deeds. Then He will have to render to me according to His own works! The greatest plenary indulgence, which is attainable by everyone, to be gained without conditions is that of Love, which covers a multitude of sins."

They said, "Surely, you will not need to pass through Purgatory; for if that were so nobody can go straight to heaven."

The Saint replied, "That does not concern me, I shall be content with God's judgement. If I should go to Purgatory, I shall walk amidst the flames like the three Hebrew adolescents in the furnace, singing the Canticle of Love!"

In heaven, you will be placed with the Seraphim, they said. "If so," she said with a smile, "I shall not copy them, for at the sight of God they cover themselves with their wings. I shall take good care not to hide myself with mine!"

When she was given a picture of St Joan of Arc being comforted in prison by her Voices, she confided, "I too, am comforted by an interior voice from above. The Saints encourage me, saying, 'As long as you are a captive in chains, you cannot fulfil your mission, but after your death will come your days of triumph.' God will do all I ask of Him in heaven because I have never done my own will here on earth."

"You will look down on us from heaven, won't you?"

"No, I will come down."

Some months before the death of Saint Therese, the life of Saint Aloysius was being read in the refectory and one of the Mothers was struck by the great affection between the young Saint and old Father Corbinelli.

"You are little Aloysius," she told Therese, "and I am Father Corbinelli, remember me when you come into the Kingdom."

"Would you like me to come down and take you there soon, dear Mother?"

"No, I have not yet suffered enough."

"No, Mother, I tell you, you have suffered quite enough." Then Mother Hermanance replied that in so grave a matter she must have the sanction of authority. The request was passed to Mother Prioress who, without making much of it, gave her sanction.

Just before she died, in the last days of her life, our Saint, scarcely able to speak in great weakness, received through the infirmarian a bouquet of flowers. It had been gathered by Mother Hermanance, who asked for a sign of affection. The message sent to Mother Hermanance said, "Tell Mother Hermanance of the Heart of Jesus, that during Mass this morning I saw Father Corbinelli's grave close to that of little Aloysius."

"That is well," sighed the good Mother, greatly touched. "Tell Sister Therese that I understand!"

She died just one year later and the two graves lie side by side – just as the Little Flower predicted!

The last words penned by the hand of Saint Therese were:

O Mary, were I Queen of Heaven and were you Therese, I would want to be Therese that I might see thee, Queen of Heaven!

***

Let us pray:

Thank you, Lord, for the Grace to see the Queen of Heaven, Mother of God, full of grace. We ask for comfort and a hand to rock us to sleep. On the night of His birth here amongst us, the Angels said:

"Glory to God in the Highest and peace to all of Goodwill." Little infant Jesus, guard and protect us whilst we play at peace with Therese. There is rejoicing in Bethlehem and Heaven that Jesus came to raise us up with Him.

Alleluia.

NB: Perhaps I am an 'old Corbinelli' whom providence has used in his dotage!

CHAPTER 14

LETTERS TO CELINE

THESE LETTERS OF SAINT THERESE WERE WRITTEN to her sister Celine, before Celine's entry into the Carmel of Lisieux in 1894. Little Therese wrote of Celine in *Earliest Memories*, the first part of her autobiographical recollections:

The last of my sisters I write about is Celine, the companion of my childhood. My memories of her are so abundant that I am in difficulty knowing what to record. We understand each other perfectly although I was much more lively and extrovert and much less tranquil and uncomplicated. Here is a letter, dear Mother, which demonstrates how much sweeter Celine was than unruly Therese. I was nearly three and Celine six and a half.

'Celine is naturally inclined to be good; as to that little puss, Therese, I cannot tell how she will turn out; she is still so young and thoughtless. She is a very intelligent child but has not the sweet disposition of her sister; her stubbornness is almost unconquerable. When she says, "No", nothing will make her change; you could leave her all day in the cellar without getting her to say "Yes". She would rather sleep there than do so.'

I had another grave fault; that of strong self-love, which Mama did not mention in her letters. Here are a couple of instances: One day Mama said, to test my pride, with a smile, "Therese, if you will kiss the ground, I will give you a halfpenny." In those days the sum was a fortune and all I had to do was to stoop down, for I was so tiny that the distance between my lips and the ground was very small. But my pride was up in arms and holding myself erect, I said, "No thank you, Mama, I will go without the halfpenny."

On another occasion, we were going into the country to see some friends. Mama told Marie to put on my prettiest frock and not to let me have bare arms. I said nothing and to all appearances was indifferent as children of that age should be, but in my mind I said, "I would look much prettier with bare arms."

With nothing but good example to follow, I see with pleasure from my Mother's letters that as I grew older, I began to be a greater comfort to her. This is what she writes in 1876.

Even Therese is anxious to practise mortification. Marie has given her little sisters a string of beads to count their acts of self-denial and they have really spiritual conversations with one another. The other day Celine asked, "How can God be in such a tiny host?" and Therese answered, "That is not difficult because God is almighty." "And what does 'Almighty' mean?" enquired Celine. "It means," said Therese, "that He can do whatever He likes." More amusing is to watch Therese putting her hand in her pocket and pull another bead along the string for every little sacrifice.

The children are inseparable and need no other company. Nurse sometimes gives Therese two bananas as presents after dinner. She and Celine then sit by the fire and play with them.

One morning Therese climbed out of her cot and got into bed with Celine. When it was time to dress her, the nurse found the little one clinging affectionately to her sister. "Oh Louise," she said, "leave me here, we are just like little bananas, you can't separate us!"

That was true. I could not bear to be away from Celine. I would rather leave my pudding unfinished than let her leave the table without me. The moment she rose from the table, I turned round in my high chair and had to be helped down at once, then we would run off to play together.

I was still too small for the long Sunday services, so Mama stayed at home to look after me. On these occasions I was very good and quiet, I would always walk about on tiptoe, but as soon as I heard the door open there was a tremendous outburst of joy. Rushing to my dear sister, I would say, "Oh Celine, give me the blessed bread, quick, quick!"

The custom still prevails in some parts of France of blessing unleavened bread at the Offertory of the Mass and then distributing to the faithful. It is known as the pain benit. That is unconsecrated bread which has been Blessed. This blessing only takes place at the Parochial Mass.

One day, she did not bring any blessed bread. I could not go without it for I looked upon this little feast as my Mass. The answer came to me, "You have no 'blessed bread', then you must make some." Celine immediately opened the larder, took out the bread, cut off a tiny piece and then said a solemn 'Hail Mary' over it. Then she gave it to me triumphantly. Making the sign of the cross, I ate it most religiously and I imagined that it tasted exactly like the real Blessed Bread.

Celine's religious name is Sister Genevieve of the Holy Face.

Letter I – dated May 1888

Dear Celine, there are moments when I wonder if I am truly in Carmel. Sometimes I can hardly believe it. What have I done for God that He should shower so many graces upon me?

A whole month has passed since we parted from one another, though even if the oceans were between us, we would always be inseparable. I know that not to have me with you is real suffering and if I listened to my desires, I should ask Jesus to let me bear your sadness. I do not listen, you see I am afraid of the temptation of desiring the better part, that is the suffering for myself. You are so right; life is often burdensome and bitter. It is hard to rise up for this daily toil especially when Jesus hides Himself from our love. What is this Sweet Friend doing? When He sees our anguish and the burdens weighing us down, why doesn't He come to our rescue and comfort us?

Do not fear little sister, He is by our side watching us and pleading for those tears. He needs them for our souls and all souls for He longs to give us a magnificent reward. I assure you that it costs Him dear to fill us with bitterness, but it is the only means of preparing us to know Him as He knows Himself and then 'to become as Gods'!

Our souls are indeed great and our destiny glorious. Let us raise ourselves up above all temporal things that pass away and keep ourselves apart from the trammelled ways of this earth! High above, the atmosphere is pure. Jesus may hide Himself but we know that He is there.

Letter II – 20th October 1888

My dearest sister, do not let your weakness make you unhappy. When in the morning, we feel that we do not have the strength for the practice of virtue, it is really a grace. It is the time to 'lay the axe to the root of the tree' **(Matthew 3: 10)** and so rely on Jesus alone. If we fall, an act of love will set all right again and Jesus smiles. He helps us without seeming to do so and the tears which sinners cause Him to shed are wiped away by the tissue of our feeble love! Love can achieve all things. The most difficult achievements 'in love' are easy and sweet. You know as well as I that our Lord does not look for great heroic deeds or even difficult accomplishments but rather for the love which alone, allows us to succeed. What then have we to fear? You desire to become a saint and ask me if this is attempting too much.

Dear Celine, I will not tell you to aim at the seraphic holiness of the most privileged souls but greater still, 'to be perfect as your Heavenly Father is perfect' **(Matthew 5: 48)**. You see, your dream and our dreams and desires are not fanciful aspirations, because Jesus Himself has commanded us to realise them.

> **Meditate.** *For it must be the aim of all Christians that they will become perfect in Christ, as perfect as the Heavenly Father. 'You must not set any limits to your love just as the Heavenly Father has no limits to His love.' Little novices of Little Therese, let us pray with absolute faith for Jesus' gift of perfect love. This gift, for which we ask, is the gift of Jesus Himself. He gives Himself, His Body and Blood, that we may love perfectly His Father, who is in heaven, and forgive, in*

His perfection, all who sin against us in Him. Therese,
you counselled your beloved sister Celine, as she cared
for your own dear father. With Celine, who surely
is in heaven with you, we ask you to come down in
perfumed prayer – that sure sign of perfect love for
Our Father who is in heaven. May the Holy Spirit fold
us in the Spirit of love, in Jesus the Christ, for it is in
Him that we love, faith points us to heaven.

Letter III – January 1889

My dear little Celine, Jesus offers you the cross, a very heavy cross, and you are afraid that you will not have the strength to carry it without falling. Be comforted, why our Beloved Himself fell three times in the dust on the way to Calvary, and why then should we not imitate our Spouse?

[This is probably a reference to the pressure on Celine who stayed at home to look after their father, who by this time had succumbed to the 'cerebral palsy' that eventually killed him.]

This is a favour from Jesus. How He must love us to send us so great a sorrow! Eternity will not last long enough for us to Bless Him for it. He heaps His favours on us as He does upon His greatest saints. What are His loving designs for our souls? That secret will only be known to us in our heavenly home on that day when 'the Lord shall wipe away all tears'.

Meditate. (Revelations 21: 1–8) *Then I saw a new*
heaven and a new earth, the first heaven and the first
earth had disappeared now and there was no longer any
sea. I saw the Holy City, the new Jerusalem, coming
down out of heaven from God, prepared as a bride
dressed for her husband. Then I heard a loud voice call
from the throne. "Look, here God lives among human

beings." He will make His home among them, they will be His people and He will be their God, "God-be-with-them." He will wipe away all tears from their eyes; there will be no more death, no more mourning or sadness or pain. The world of the 'past' has gone. Now we have nothing more to hope for on earth. 'The cool evenings have passed' for us, only suffering remains. Ours is a happy allotment and the Seraphim in Heaven envy our happiness!

The other day, I came across this remarkable passage. 'It is not the same thing to be resigned and to be united to the will of God. There is the same disparity between them as that which exists between union and unity. In union, there are still two objects, in unity there is only one.'

Yes, let us be one with God, even in this life, and in order to be so, we should be not just resigned, we should embrace the Cross with joy.

Meditate. *Resignation is passive acceptance; love is our will in action.*

Letter IV – 8th February 1889

My dear little sister, Jesus is 'a spouse of blood' **(Exodus 4: 25).** He desires for His meeting place, the valve spring of our hearts. You are so right; it costs us dear to give Him what He asks. But what joy, whatever the cost! It is happiness to carry our crosses and to know our weaknesses as we do so.

Let us not complain to Our Lord of the Cross, for the crosses He sends us. I cannot divine the immensity of infinite love, which has led Him to pamper us in this way. Our dear father must indeed be loved by God to have so much suffering given to him! I realise that it is by humiliation alone, that saints are made and I know that our trial is a mine of gold for us to build on account. I am a little grain of sand yet I want to set to work, though I lack both the courage and the strength. No, you see, my very weakness makes my task easier for I will work with and for love alone. Our martyrdom is beginning. Let us go on to suffer together, dear sister. Let us offer our sufferings to Jesus for the salvation of souls.

> **Meditate.** *In our weakness, Lord, in your love, we grow strong. For you are our strength and out of the strong, in the weakness of death, came forth the sweetness of life. (Tate & Lyle Syrup tin!)*

> **Meditate.** *"He is my Blood Bridegroom for I have circumcised my heart that it should be a tender loving garden just for Him."*

Letter V – 12th March 1889

I must forget this world. Here all things weary me. I have only one source of Joy, it is my suffering. This Joy which does not come from pleasure through the senses, is above all, such ephemeral happiness.

Life is passing and eternity comes ever closer. Soon we shall live the life of God. After we have drunk from the springs of bitterness then our thirst will be satisfied at the fountain of sweetness.

'Because the world as we know it is passing away' **(1 Corinthians 7: 31)**, soon we shall behold new skies. A brighter sun will light with its gentle splendour, crystal seas and infinite horizons. We shall no longer be held prisoner in a land of exile;

all this will have passed away. With our heavenly spouse we will move over a shoreless ocean.

Now 'our harps are hanging on the willows which grow by the rivers of Babylon'. **(Psalms 137)**

On the day of our deliverance what harmonies will they bring forth, how joyfully will all the strings vibrate! Now 'we weep, remembering Zion, for how can we sing the songs of the Lord in exile?' **(Psalms 137)**

The theme of our song is suffering for Jesus offers us the chalice of the blood of His passion. Let us drink from it and know the sublimity of His peace. He who gives us peace, does not say 'I give you joy', at least not the joy of this shallow life. The joy of our will is doing His will and we will only suffer then, peace in Him. We cannot enjoin love without suffering for our nature is defiant and must be encountered in this life. We suffer in this battle of nature so that great treasures come within our reach. Indeed this contest is our fight for life. It is so precious that Jesus came down on earth with the purpose of possessing it. Of course, we would like to suffer nobly and generously and never fall. What an illusion! What does it matter if I fall at any moment! In that way I know my weakness and this knowledge is a considerable gain. My God, you know what little good I can accomplish outside the embrace of your divine embrace. If you leave me on my own it is because you delight in my infant struggles to reach for you. Knowing this, I am not troubled at all. If you are willing to hold in peace the trial of not being pleased with yourself, you will be offering the Divine Master a home in your heart.

Even so, you will suffer because you will be a stranger in your own home. Do not be afraid, the poorer you are the more will Jesus love you! I know that He is more pleased to see you struggle in the night along a stony road than walking in daylight along a path carpeted by flowers, because the flowers might engross you and delay your progress.

> **Meditate.** *Let us make haste to the Lord without distraction, for we are going home to be clothed in His light. For He awaits the prodigal with open arms and prepares a banquet for sinners who have come home.*

Letter VI – 14th July 1889

My darling sister, I am ever with you in Spirit. It is the Lord living here on earth, but tomorrow, no, in an hour, we shall be at rest.

O my God, what then shall we see? What is this life which will then have no end? Our Lord will be the Soul of our soul. Oh, unfathomable mystery! 'What no eye has seen and no ear heard, what the mind of man cannot grasp, all this God has prepared for those who love Him.' All this will come to be very soon, very soon, if we love Jesus with our whole heart. It is clear to me that God has no need for years to perfect his labour of love in a soul. One shining ray from His heart can, in an instant, make His flower burst into blossom and never fade. Celine, during these fleeting moments left to us, let us save souls! I know in my heart that our Spouse asks us to bring Him souls, above all the souls of priests. It is He who calls me to tell you this.

There is only one thing to be done here below; to love Jesus and to save souls for Him that He may be more and more loved. We must not let pass the slightest opportunity of giving Him joy. We must refuse Him nothing. He is in such need of love.

We are His chosen lilies and He dwells here as King amongst us. We share the honour of His royal nature, His divine blood is dewdrops on our petals and His crown of thorns releases the perfume of our love as they pierce us.

> **Meditate.** *The blood of His passion fills the rosebud of our hearts. He draws us into the eternal flame of His Sacred Heart. He seeks us, His Beloved, and we, His Beloved, seek our Beloved, our life in the home of His heart. This unity of love is the Spirit He sent us.*

Letter VII – 22nd October 1889

My dearest Celine, I send you a picture of the Holy Face. The contemplation of this adorable countenance belongs, in a special way, to my sister, truly the sister of my soul. May she be another Veronica and wipe away all the blood, sweat and tears of Jesus, her only love. May she win souls for Him. May she force her way through the hostile escort that is the world that hems us in, to come close to His side. Happy will you be when she sees in heaven, the value of that draught with which she quenched the thirst of her heavenly spouse. She will see those parched lips and hear the parched throat speaking to her that one eternal word, Love, the thanks that has no end. 'Let the sons of Israel say, His love has no end.'

Goodbye, little Veronica, tomorrow without doubt, your Beloved will ask some new sacrifice, some fresh release from His thirst. 'Let us go and die with Him.'

NB: Celine, after their father's death, entered the Carmel of Lisieux as Sister Genevieve of the Holy Face and after the Saint's death, in 1898 she produced a wonderful painting of the photograph produced from the Turin Shroud. Celine devoted six months to this holy task of love and Pius X attached many indulgences to this portrait of the Holy Face and expressed his desire that it should find a place of honour in every Catholic household. He also granted an indulgence of three hundred days for the recitation of the prayer to the Holy Face composed by the Saint.

An Act of Consecration
to the Holy Face
(For us novices)

O, adorable face of Jesus, you have made a special choice of our souls in order to give yourself to them. We come to consecrate our souls to you. Jesus, we seem to hear you say, "Open to me, my sisters, my spouses, for my face is wet with dew and my locks with drops of the night." Our souls understand your language of love. We desire to wipe your sweet face and to console you for the contempt of the wicked. You are still hidden from their eyes. They look upon you as an object of contempt.

O Blessed Face, more lovely than the lilies and the roses of Spring. You are not hidden from us. The tears, which mist up your eyes, are as precious as pearls, which we gather up with delight. It is through their infinite value that we purchase the souls of our brothers. From your adorable lips we have heard that cry, "I thirst."

We know this thirst which pervades you is a thirst for Love! To quench it, we desire to possess an infinite love. Dear spouse of our souls, if we could love with the love of all hearts that love would be yours. Give us, O Lord, this love then come to your spouses and satisfy your thirst!

Give to us souls, we thirst for souls, above all, for the souls of Apostles and martyrs that we may, through them, inflame all poor sinners with love of thee. O adorable face, we shall succeed in winning this grace from you without thought of our exile, 'by the rivers of Babylon'.

We will sing softly the sweetest melodies because you are the one true home of our souls. 'Our songs will not be sung in a land of exile.' O beloved face of Jesus, whilst we await the eternal day when we shall gaze upon your infinite Glory, our desire is to delight your divine eyes by keeping our faces hidden so that, on earth, we shall not be recognised. Dear Jesus, Heaven is for us your Hidden Face.

Meditate. To see Him is to be perfect in truth, perfect in love in the light of all perfection; for to see Him is to see the Father and the Spirit of their love. Holy Spirit, where you live may we know Him as He is, for to know Him is to know Our Father in Heaven.

Letter VIII – 18th July 1890

My dear petite sister, I send you a passage from Isaiah to comfort you. Long ago, the prophet was filled, as our souls are today, with the thought of the hidden beauties of the Divine Face. Many centuries have passed since then. I wonder then, what is time?

Time is a mirage, it is a dream. Already, God beholds us in glory and rejoices in our everlasting bliss. So much goodness comes to me with this thought. I understand now why He allows us to suffer!

Since our Beloved has trodden the winepress above, the winepress which provides His saving cup from which we drink, we cannot then refuse to be clothed in His bloodstained garments or to tread with Him, the new wine which we will drink with Him.

When He looks around, He will not be able to say, 'there was no one to help me'. Nor will He say, 'I was appalled but could find no supporter' **(Isaiah 63: 5)**. We shall be there to help Him!

'He was despised, the lowest of mankind, a man of sorrows, familiar with suffering on whom we looked away, for Him we had no regard' **(Isaiah 53: 3)**. Alas, it is so even to this day and no one has compassion or understands His tears. 'Open to me, my sister, my spouse,' He says to us, 'for my head is bathed in dew and my locks the drops of the night.'

Thus Jesus cries out to us when He is deserted and forgotten. To be forgotten, this gives Him so much pain! Our dear father, it is heart-rending, yet how can we weep since Our Lord Himself was looked upon, 'While we thought of Him as someone being punished and struck with affliction by God'? **(Isaiah 53: 4)**

In this great sorrow at our loss, we should forget ourselves and pray for priests, our lives must be devoted to them. Our Divine Master makes me feel more and more that this is what He asks us to do.

> **Meditate.** *On 29th July 1894, God called their saintly father to Himself. As he suffered but loved much, we recall his little Queen who loved in her suffering the Holy Face caressed by Veronica. We too, long to look upon that Face of Our Saviour and the Saviour of all. They suffer naught that suffer here and are rewarded with eternal fitness.*
>
> *BWF*

CHAPTER 15

HER FATHER IN HEAVEN

AS WE CONTINUE TO MEDITATE UPON THESE letters to her elder sister Celine, we smell the perfume of their intense unity. The bonds of affection in childhood as loving Catholic Christians, within Holy Marriage, where a little flock was nurtured within that inseparable union of love between Louis Joseph and Zelie Martin. We know they are in heaven together, intense and happy, absorbed in their childhood pursuits where play and prayer and meditation are all at one. Joined in the Trinitarian unity of love where all is perfection, joy, light, love and truth. They are in Paradise with Jesus and the penitent thief, crucified next to Jesus on the Cross. We ask to follow them and offer our lives to Him, Our Saviour. Thus are we crucified with Him in this life, offering through Him all our failings and little triumphs, for in Him, the perfect offering, we are acceptable to God.

Thus part of the Good News revealed through Saint Paul is, we rejoice in Christ and long to be crucified with Him on the Cross – the Cross of life, for it was from the Cross that Jesus died and descended, arose and Ascended into heaven. This is why we understand that our lives here resemble His passion, for we too, must die and descend to rise again in Him, in His resurrection and meet Him coming on the clouds, for His judgement, before He leads us into Heaven.

Letter IX – 23rd September 1890

Oh Celine, what a wound of love I have received! It has, I know, been inflicted by a loving hand, by a hand of jealous love. All was ready for my espousal. (Little Therese was professed on 8th September 1890 and received the veil on 24th September.) You know that something most special was needed at this feast. It is true that Jesus had already adorned me with many jewels, yet there was one of incomparable beauty still missing; this priceless diamond He has given me today. Papa will not be here tomorrow!

Celine, I confess that I have cried bitterly – I am still crying and I can scarcely hold my pen. You know how intensely I longed to see our dearest Father again. No, I am convinced that it is God's will that he should not be at my feast. God has permitted it simply to try our love. Jesus desires that I will be an orphan to be alone, with Him alone, so that He may unite Himself more closely to me. He will give all this back to me in heaven; this joy which He has lawfully taken and which He has denied me here on earth.

Today, this trial is one of those intense sorrows that are most difficult to understand. A joy was set before us most natural and simple to be fulfilled. We stretched out our hands to receive this treasured gift and this coveted, longed-for joy was taken from our grasp.

It is not the hand of man that has done this thing; it is God's work. Please try to understand your Therese and let us accept this cross which is offered cheerfully with good heart.

Tomorrow's feast will be one of tears but I know that Jesus will be greatly consoled.

> **Meditate.** *Console us, Jesus, wipe away our tears; you are near and comfort us. In your arms we can rest while suffering engulfs us here on earth. You will restore all goodness and then all things will be well, for you are Our Saviour, our Brother, our Friend, the Alpha and Omega of all creation.*
> *Alleluia!*

Letter X – 14th October 1890

My darling Sister, I feel and know your suffering, its intensity and its smothering presence in your heart. I realise your terrible anguish and I share it. If only I could impart to you the peace which Jesus has put into my soul in the midst of this most bitter travail. Be comforted, all things will pass away! Our vivid lives of yesterday are spent; death too will come and go. Then we shall rejoice in life, true life, for countless ages, for evermore!

Meanwhile we must make our hearts a garden of delights where our Sweet Saviour may come and take His rest. Let us plant lilies there and in harmony with St John of the Cross, say:

There I stayed in deep obscurity my head resting upon the breast of Him I love. Lost to myself and all else in the Universe I emptied all my cares away and left them discarded where the lilies grow.

> **Meditate.** *Let us retire from this world into deep, deep prayer. Prayer beyond the rush of words, forced by despair. Let our prayer be love in action that needs*

no word. Let us recline beside Him, as Beloved, and rest our heads upon His chest. Then our breathing and our hearts will beat in unison and like the faithful lily, perfumed pure, grow in silence with our rested feet washed there. Then our cares like brown, dead leaves will form a compost in the lily fields of our hearts and we will arise and go gaily in His commandment of love. For we can love the dead and those yet born. We can still love Him and know that we are loved by those gone on. They are only just a little way ahead and at the summit He waits with open arms for all us happy pilgrims embraced in His bond of love.

Alleluia, Alleluia!

Letter XI – 26th April 1891

My dear little Sister, Three years ago our hearts had not yet been so badly bruised and life was still one glad smile! Then Jesus beheld us from above and all things were changed into an ocean of soft, soft tears. That ocean is also an ocean of grace and love. God has taken to Himself, taken away from us, him whom we loved so tenderly. I wonder, was it so that we could say more truly than ever, 'Our Father, who art in heaven'?

How consoling are these divine words and what vast horizons, vistas of love, they open before us.

My darling Celine, who asked me so many questions when we were little, why is it you never asked, "Why has God not made me an angel?" Well, I shall tell you. Our Lord desires to establish His court of the Kingdom of heaven, here on earth. He needs for this both angel-martyrs and angel-Apostles. He has not made you an angel in heaven because He needs you to be an angel on earth, so that you may be able to suffer within

His love.

Dearest of sisters, the shadows are drawing in; the rays of the Eternal Sun are thawing this hoar frost of winter. Just a little while longer and we shall be in our true country and our childhood joys, those ecstatic Sunday evenings, those jewelled outpourings of our hearts, will be given back to us forever.

Letter XII – 15th August 1891

My dear little Sister, to write to you today, I am obliged to steal some time from Our Lord. He will forgive me because we are going to talk about Him together. The immense solitude and calm beauty of the picturesque landscapes which spread themselves out before you, ought to lift up your soul in a fountain of light! I am not blessed with such visions; I must content myself by saying with St John of the Cross, in his spiritual canticles:

> *'In Christ I have the mountains*
> *the quiet wooded valleys.'*

Meditate. *Immense and marvellous is the beauty of His works. From the secluded arbour of His love to the deep blue sky above, from the dewpond on the downland heights to the roistering oceans of North and South. From black forested wastes to the orchards and harvest fields of France. This quilted sleeve of creation clothes us in His blanket love. The beautiful goodness of creation speaks of His love. Celine painted a portrait of His Holy Face and with her sister lived in His waterfall of grace.*

Amen.

Behold us, Lord, pilgrims at your feet. Here we are, scattered petals, in a heap. A heap of love, sprinkled with your blood, Novices of your treasure, Saint Therese.

BWF.

Recently I have begun to think of those things I could undertake for the salvation of souls. These plain words from the Gospels have illuminated my thoughts (John 4: 34–39):

My food is to do the will of the One who sent me and to complete His work. Do the Samaritans not have a saying: 'Four months and then the harvest'? Well I tell you, look about you, look at the fields: already they are white, ready for harvest. Already the reaper is being paid his wages; already he is bringing in grain for eternal life. So the sower and reaper can rejoice together. For here the proverb holds true, one sows, another reaps. I sent you to reap a harvest you have not laboured for. Others have laboured for it and you have come into the rewards of their labour.

Here we have a mystery! Is not Jesus all-powerful? Do not creatures belong to Him, who made them? Why does He then ask of us, 'I send you to reap a harvest you did not labour for'? It is because the delicate nature of His love is beyond our poor understanding. He desires that we share intimately with Him, all that He does! The Creator of the Universe waits upon the prayer of a poor little soul, to save a multitude of souls, ransomed like her, at the cost of His own blood.

Jesus once said to His disciples, 'the harvest is great indeed but the labourers are few, pray therefore, to the Lord of the harvest, that He sends out labourers.' **(Matthew 9: 37–38)**

Our vocation is not to go out and reap in our Father's fields. Jesus does not say, 'bend down and reap the Harvest'. Our mission is yet more sublime. "Look around and see," He tells us, "see, how in Heaven, there are empty thrones. It is for you to fill them; you are like Moses, praying on the mountain; so ask me for labourers and they shall be sent. I only await a prayer, a sigh!"

Is not the Apostleship of prayer, in one sense, higher than the spoken word? It is for us, through prayer, to train workers who will spread the good news of the Gospel and who will save countless souls – the souls to whom we shall be spiritual mothers. What then have we to envy in the Priests of the Lord?

Letter XIII

My dear little sister, the gentle affection of our childhood has matured into the closest union of heart and mind. Jesus has reached out and drawn us to Him together, for you have always been His. He placed the world beneath our feet, for like Zaccheus, we have climbed the tree to see Him coming. That lofty, mysterious tree from where we can say, 'All is mine, all is for me, the earth and the heavens are mine. God Himself is mine and the Mother of my God is for me'. (St John of the Cross.)

> **Meditate.** *He has placed the world under our feet for it is His footstool and He lifts us up to Him in His arms. That lofty mysterious tree, the tree of life, is the Cross. He was lifted up on the Cross, to take*

> *away all sins. From the spiritual heights, we look upon*
> *'His footstool' as our library ladder where we mount,*
> *in Him, the stairway to heaven. This is the treasure*
> *house of the Church's communion of faith because His*
> *mysterious body is the Church, at the heart of which*
> *is little Therese's 'little way of love'. The collaborative*
> *communion, the ministry of the emulation of the Child*
> *Jesus, humble in quiet, free obedience to His Father,*
> *Saint Joseph and Mary, the Mother of God.*

Speaking of that Blessed Mother, I must tell you of one of my simple ways. Sometimes I hear myself saying to her, 'Dearest Mother, it appears that I am happier than you. I have you for my mother and you have no Blessed Virgin to love. It is true that you are the Mother of Jesus but you have given Him to me. Also, from the Cross He has given you to be our Mother – thus we are richer than you! Long ago, out of humility, you longed to be the handmaid, the Mother of God. I, your poor little creature, am not your handmaid but your child. You are the Mother of Jesus and also my Mother. Dear Celine, Jesus revealed for us, many mysteries, by urging us to climb the mystical tree of life as I said above. What new knowledge is He teaching us now? Has He not taught us already, all His secrets?

Through Zaccheus, He teaches us, 'He looked up and said to him, "Zaccheus, come down and hurry because I am going to stay at your house today."' Jesus commands us to come down. Where must we go? 'The Jews asked Him, "Master, where do you live?" He said to them, "The foxes have holes and the birds of the air, nests, but the Son of Man has nowhere to lay his head."' If we are to join Him in His 'dwelling place', we must go down and be so poor that we, too, have nowhere to lay our heads.

Our Lord desires that we receive Him into our hearts and no doubt, they are inhabited by others. Alas mine is not empty of self. That is why He commands me to come down to the ground so that Jesus will find a resting place for His divine head and know that there, at least, He is loved and understood.

> **Meditate.** *In the dust and mire, even in the foulness of the trench of warfare, He will be found. The perfection of His presence inspiring love even in His smallness, 'the white host of His presence'. He is present in the darkest darkness, for He descended into hell. His saving grace given for all, sufficient unto all, for He is Son of Man, Son of God, the Saviour of all. Where He is, let us gladly follow, to serve Him, the Servant of God.*

Letter XIV – 25th April 1893

My little Celine, I must come to you and disclose Jesus' desires with regard to your soul. Recall His words. He did not say, 'I am the flower of the gardens, a carefully tended rose'. On the contrary He said, 'I am the flower of the fields and the lily of the valleys'. **(Song of Songs 2: 1)** Rejoice, you must always be like a pearl drop of dew hidden in the petal cup of this Lily.

The dewdrop – what is more pure or perfect? It is not born from the clouds; it is born beneath a starry sky and stays just one day. When the sun projects its piercing rays, these delicate pearls, adorning each blade of grass, vanish into the rising mists of dawn. There is the portrait of little Celine! She is a single pendant of dew, heaven born, her true home. Through the night of this life, she must hide away in the Flower of the Field's golden cup; they must never see her perfumed place of rest. Happy dewdrop known only to God, take no notice of the tumultuous currents of this world! Do not envy the clear stream winding among the meadows. The murmur of its flowing waters may be most sweet but it is for the ears of His creatures. The Flower of the Field could not fold it in its cup. One must be lowly to draw near to Jesus and there are too few souls that long to be lowly and unknown. 'They argue, the river and the brook are far more useful than the dewdrop in the order of Creation. What use is one dewdrop? Its only purpose is to refresh just one Flower of the Field for a brief moment'.

They do not know the true Flower of the Field. If they knew Him, then they would better understand Our Lord's reproach to Martha. Our Beloved does not need our beautiful deeds or our perfumed thoughts. If He needed lofty ideas He has the Angels whose knowledge far surpasses that of the greatest genius on earth. He has come among us not to seek intellectual or other talents. He has come as the Flower of the Field, as a sign of His love of simplicity.

The lily of the valley invites just one dewdrop, which will rest in His petalled centre for just one night, hidden from human sight. However, when the shadows begin to fade, when the Flower of the Field becomes the Light of Justice, then the dewdrop, the humble sharer of His home and of His exile, will rise up in Him as the vapour of love. He will gild her with His radiant light, before the whole court of heaven. She will shine eternally, a precious pearl, a dazzling image of the Divine Sun.

Letter XV – 15th August 1893

My Dear Celine, What you have written fills me with joy; you are journeying by the Royal Road.

The spouse of the Canticles, unable to find her Beloved in the evening, went into the city to find Him. It was a fruitless journey; only outside the walls could she find him. It is not in the calmness of repose that Jesus demands that we seek Him and discover His presence. He cloaks Himself in the mystery of darkness. This was not His way with the multitude because they were moved to revere Him even as He spoke to them. The weaker souls He charmed and delighted with His eloquence. This was to strengthen them against the day of temptation and trial. Nonetheless, His faithful friends were few that day when 'He was silent' **(Matthew 26: 63)**, in the presence of those in judgement on Him.

What a sublime melody in my heart is that silence of the Divine Master, the Lamb of God. He wants us to give Him alms as we give to the poor and He places Himself in our mercy. He will take nothing not given fondly; the smallest trifle is precious in His Divine eyes. He holds His hand open to receive our meagre gift of love, so that, on that glorious day of judgement we may hear those ineffable words: 'Come you Blessed of my Father, for I was hungry and you gave me something to eat, thirsty and you gave me something to drink. I was a stranger and you took me in, sick and you visited me, in prison and you came to me.' **(Matthew 25: 34–36)**

Dearest Celine, let us rejoice in our lot. Let us give and give again, give generously, never in doubt that our Beloved is a hidden treasure which few know how to find. To discover what is hidden, we must enter into the hiding place. May our life be one long concealment. The author of the *Imitation of Christ* writes: 'If you want to know and learn something of great moment, then let your love be hidden and be esteemed as a lowly one. Having forsaken all things, then forsake yourself. One man may glory in this and another in that, but you rejoice neither in this nor that, but in contempt for yourself.'

> **Meditate.** *To be perfect give up all for Him, for He is perfect. Then with Him only and all else given away, His perfection will be your perfection, only then will we come to Our Father in Heaven.*

Letter XVI

My Dear Celine, I am pleased that my letters are of some help but I am under no illusion. 'Unless the Lord build the house, they labour in vain who build.' The finest eloquence cannot impel a single act of love unless grace touches the heart.

Behold the peach with its delicate rosy tint, with its fullness of honeyed nectar beyond the skills of man to invent. Is it for the peach's sake that God created the colour so beautiful to the eye, that velvety skin so soft to touch? Is it for itself He made it so luscious? No, it is for us; the only created thing that is all its own and essential to its being as a peach, is its kernel: it possesses nothing beyond this. Thus also, it pleases Jesus to lavish His gifts on certain souls in order to draw others to Himself. In His mercy, He humbles them inwardly and with gentleness compels them to know their nothingness and His almighty power. Now this innate sense of humility is like a kernel of grace which God develops for that Blessed day, when clothed with an imperishable beauty, they will be placed in safety on the banqueting table of Paradise.

Dear little sister, sweet echo of my soul, Therese is far from the heights of fervour. When I am in this state of spiritual dryness, unable to pray or practise virtue, I look for little opportunities, the smallest trifles to give pleasure to Jesus: a smile or a kind word, for instance, when I want to be silent or show that I am bored. If I find no such occasion, I repeat over and over again that I love Him. This is not hard and it kindles the flame of love in my heart. Even if that fire of love seems dead, I would drop my tiny straws on the ashes and I am confident that they would flame up again. It is true that I am not always faithful but I never lose courage. I place myself in the arms of the Lord. He teaches me 'to extract profit from all things, from the good and from the bad which He finds in me'. **(St John of the Cross)** He teaches me to invest in the bank of love, or rather it is He who invests for me, without divulging how, He does it and that is His affair and not mine. I just surrender myself to Him without reserve, without any idea of what return it will bring me. For I am not the prodigal child. Jesus need not trouble about a feast for me, for I am always with Him. **(Luke 15: 31)** It is most touching to read in the Gospel how the good shepherd leaves the faithful of his flock on the hillside, to hasten after the lost sheep. He is sure of them. For how could they stray, for they are prisoners of love? So it is that the beloved Shepherd of our souls deprives us of His presence to give His consolations to sinners. Or if He leads us to Mount Tabor, it is for a brief moment. The pastureland is in the valleys; 'it is there that He takes His rest at midday'. **(Canticle of Canticles i.e. Song of Songs.)**

> **Meditate.** *The beauty, the wonders, the delights of this world; He made for us. Beauty and melody,*

perfume and the silken surface, we enjoy, taste, see how sweet is the Lord. Not for itself or for Himself, but for humankind, He fashioned the stars, the woods, the sunlit dawn. Even the snow wastes and the desert He made beautiful for us. From birdsong to the sheep on the slope. All the animal kingdom delights our eye. His grace is like the mountain stream. From the heights of His love it surges down into the valley of our hearts. So the garden blooms in His sunlight and we play upon the harp, the instrument of His Spirit of Love. The wind of His breath moves the strings of love in our hearts.

Alleluia.

BWF.

Chapter 16

Celine Comes to Carmel

THERESE REVEALS TO US, AS IT WAS revealed to her, the great honour and privilege it is to be a human being, body and soul made by God, sustained in life by the Holy Spirit of Love and created through Jesus, Son of God, and redeemed to salvation through His Life, death and resurrection, Son of Man.

To become sons and daughters of God through Him in love is a process of perfection. The material forms and conglomerates of phenomena of this world pass away in us through death when the physical separates in this form of our mortal frame and is resurrected with the material substance immersed in and reformed as spiritual beings.

The substance of all matter is particles of light formed as quark to anti-quark, attracted and repelled, held in a unity by the sign of light in pulsing, waving particles of the light of the Creator's love for all in His Creation.

Thus we are Blessed, separated from Him our Spouse, the Beloved, only by the tent frame of our mortal being. Even here, in this tent of clay, He has joined us in the Incarnation, Son of Man, Jesus the Christ; His presence here revealed in the reality of His substance in the appearance of bread and wine, the physical substance of His presence.

In the spontaneity of our spiritual childhood, we rest on His shoulder, held close in His arms, those arms stretched wide from the Cross. In this unity of love, salvation flows in the Sacraments of the Church, the sevenfold fountain of our redemption.

Letter XVII – 20th October 1893

My dear sister, In the *Canticle of Canticles* **(Song of Songs 7: 1)**, there is this passage – which applies so aptly to you. 'What do you see in your Beloved? – Surely a band of musicians in an armed camp.'

Through suffering, your life has become a battlefield and as on any battlefield, there must be a band of musicians. You will be the little harp of Jesus. No concert band is complete without a singer and when Jesus plays, then Celine joins in the melody with her voice. For as His little harp you sing divinely. When the music is sorrowing, she will sing songs of exile and when it is gay, she will, sing in counterpoint, the music of Paradise.

Whatever may happen, all events here on earth, joyful or sad, are just passing events unable to provoke a single vibration from the harp of Jesus. He alone has the right to gently pluck those strings.

It is a delight to remember that great saint Cecilia. She is a great example to us! She lived in a pagan world in the heart of danger. At the moment she was to marry a man whose love was so base, I recall that she should have trembled and wept in fear. However, during the celebration of their wedding, Cecilia kept singing in her heart! [Office of Saint Cecilia] What perfect resignation! Without doubt, she heard other melodies not of this earth. Her divine spouse, He too was singing and the angels responded in chorus with the music of Bethlehem's Blessed night, 'Glory to God in the highest and peace to men of goodwill on earth'.

The Glory of God – Cecilia understood it so well and longed for it in her heart. She knew intuitively that her Jesus was thirsting for souls and that is the reason and her whole desire, to bring her young Roman whose only thought was of earthly glory, to Him quickly. This wise virgin will make him a martyr and multitudes will follow in his footsteps. She has no fear for the angels at Bethlehem promised peace. The Prince of Peace is her protection to guard her virginity and give her just recompense. 'How lovely are the lives of the chaste.'

Dearest sister, I am hardly conscious of what I write – my pen follows the impulse of my heart. You tell me that you are aware of your weakness but rather that is grace. It is Our Lord who sows the seeds of self-distrust in your soul. Do not fear! You do not give Him pleasure in small things then He will be obliged to help you in great things.

The Apostles laboured alone throughout the night; they toiled and caught nothing. Their labours were acceptable to Him. However He demonstrated to them that He is the provider of all things. First however, He asked for an act of humility. "Brothers, have you caught any fish?" Saint Peter replied in helpless frustration, "Master, we have toiled all night and caught nothing." The heart of Jesus was touched deeply. Had the Apostle made some small catch, perhaps Our Divine Master would not have worked the miracle. They had caught nothing but soon, through the power of God's goodness, his nets were full of fine fish. God gives with Divine generosity but He insists on humility of the heart.

Letter XVIII – 7th July 1894

My dear little sister, I do not know if you are still in the same frame of mind when you wrote to me last. I am going to presume that you are. My reply is this passage of the *Canticle of Canticles*, which explains so well the state of a soul in arid parchedness, a soul deprived of joy and consolation in anything. 'I went down into the garden of nut trees to see the fruits of the valleys and to see if the vineyard was flourishing and if the pomegranates were in bud. I no longer knew where I was. My soul was troubled and I felt desolate as if the Chariots of Aminadab had passed through'.

This is a true illustration of the state of our souls. Often we go down into the lush valleys and vast fields of Holy Scripture where our hearts long to find nourishment – these places, which so often provided us with the yield of the richest treasures of the harvest – only to find an arid waterless waste. We are lost, not knowing where we are. Instead of peace and light, all is sorrow and darkness. Like the Spouse in the Canticles, we know the cause of this trial – 'My soul was troubled by the destruction of the Chariots of Aminadab'. We are not yet at home in our true country. As gold is refined in the furnace, so our souls are tested by temptation. 'The Chariots' are the idle clamours which fill our senses and beset us and disturb us. Are they interior troubles or exterior events? We cannot tell, only Jesus knows. He sees all our grief and in the darkness suddenly, His voice is heard. 'Return, return, Shulamite, come back that we may behold you!' **(Song of Songs 6: 12)** What a call of grace! We could no longer look upon ourselves; the sight filled us with dread. Yet Jesus calls us that He may gaze upon us at His leisure. He wills to see us. He comes and with Him are the other two persons of the Adorable Trinity, to take possession of our souls. Our Lord promised this, He said of old with sublime tenderness, "If anyone loves me, he will keep my Word and my Father will love him and we will come and make our home in him." To keep the Word of Jesus is the one absolute condition of our ultimate happiness. The proof of our love for Him and His Word for us , is His very self, for He is the uncreated Word of the Father.

In the Gospel of John, we hear His own sublime prayer, 'Sanctify them in truth. Thy Word is Truth'. In another passage, Jesus teaches us that He is 'the Way, the Truth and the Life'. We know then what is the nature of the Word which must be kept. We cannot ask as Pilate did, 'What is truth?' We possess the Truth for our Beloved lives in our hearts!

Often this Beloved is a sachet of myrrh. We drink the chalice of His sufferings, but how sweet it will be on the day we hear these gentle words, 'You are those who kept watch with me in my temptations. I give then, to you, just as my Father has given me, His Kingdom.'

Letter XIX – 19th August 1894

This may be the last time that I will have to write to you in order to discourse with you, my dear little sister. God, in His goodness, has granted my dearest wish. Come and we shall suffer together … then Jesus will call one of us and the other will remain in exile yet a little longer. Now listen carefully to what I am going to say. God will never separate us and if I die before you, do not think that I will be far away. No, we shall be even more closely united. You must not grieve at my childish prophecy. I am not ill, I have an iron constitution but the Lord can break iron as if it were clay! Our dear father made his presence known in a way which touches me deeply!

After a living death of five long years, what joy it is to find him as he used to be; now he is more a father to me than ever. How well he is going to repay you for the love and care you so generously gave to him. You were his angel, now he is your angel. He has only been one month in heaven and already through his intercession, all your plans are succeeding. It is easy now for him to arrange matters for us. He had much less to suffer on Celine's account than he had for his poor little queen. For a long time you have been asking me for news about the noviciate, especially about my duties, and now I am going to satisfy you.

In my dealings with the novices, I am like a setter on the scent of game. This task gives me much anxiety because it is so exacting. All day long from morning to nightfall, I am in pursuit of game. Mother Prioress and the Novice Mistress play the part of sportsmen. However, sportsmen are too big to move through the cover unnoticed, whereas a little dog can push its way anywhere and its scent is so keen! I keep a close watch on my little rabbits, I do not want to hurt them so I tell them softly, "You must keep your fur glossy and not look foolishly around like a rabbit of the warren." Indeed, I try to make them just as the Hunter of Souls would want them – simple creatures that go on browsing busily without regard to anything else. I smile as I write, but in all seriousness I am convinced that one of these rabbits – you know which one I mean – is worth a hundred times more than the setter. It has passed through many dangers and I admit that had I been in its place, I should long since have been lost forever in the great forest of the world.

Meditate. *As novices, taught by our Novice Mistress, we listen to the Word, the Word of God that buoys us up and leads us to the pastures of His Heart. Sacred Heart of Jesus, fill us like Little Therese, with love and compassion and joy in all that we experience here on earth. Saint Therese, little setter of heaven, watch over us.*

Letter XX – September 1894

Dearest Celine, I rejoice that you are not elated at the thought of entering Carmel. This is a sign of Our Lord's favour; it reveals that He seeks a precious gift from your hands. He knows how much sweeter it is to give than to receive. What happiness it is to suffer for Him who loves us even unto folly and then to pass for fools in this world! Men judge others in the light of their own understanding and as their understanding does not prevail in reason, then it judges us unreasonable.

We can console ourselves that we are not alone in this. Folly was the only crime with which Herod could reproach Our Lord and Herod was right. It was folly indeed, for the King of Glory who sits above the Cherubim and Seraphim, to seek out thrones for Himself in poor human hearts. Was He not supremely happy in the company of His Father and the Holy Spirit of Love? Why then did He come down from heaven to earth to search out us sinners and make us His closest friends? No, our folly cannot ever exceed the foolishness of Christ and our actions are eminently reasonable compared with His incarnation. The world may ignore us and vilify us. I repeat, it is the world that is insane because it will not take note of what Jesus has done and how He suffered to save the world from eternal damnation.

> **Meditate.** *The wind sighs on the heights. The poor open their hands to share in the bounty of His creative care. Our Saviour resides in the Sanctuary where His grace flows full as the ocean's roar. What is there worthy of our little love? Only Him who in ignominy, died upon the Cross, For All.*
>
> *BWF.*

We are not idlers or spendthrifts. Our Divine Master has taken our defence upon Himself. Remember the scene in the house of Lazarus: Martha, serving whilst Mary had no thought for food. Her only thought was how she might please her Beloved and also when she 'broke her alabaster box, pouring out upon her Saviour's head, the precious spikenard and the house was filled with the odour of His sanctity. The Apostles murmured against Mary, just as men murmur against us. Even fervent Catholics believe our way to be exaggerated and that we ought to be busy like Martha, instead of pouring out upon Him the perfumed moments of our lives. What does it matter if the ointment jars are broken since Our Lord is consoled and the world can, in spite of itself, take joy in the perfume that fills the house. It has a great need for this perfume, the sure sign of the distillation of His perfection to purify the polluted air they breathe. Note these passages from the Gospel are today understood as quite separate acts by two different people called Mary. This may not have been so in the time of Saint Therese. However her conflation here of the narratives makes the point of her teaching thus: Christ needs our personal love and acts of our generosity and understanding of His incarnate suffering which continues as our sins wound Him. Good works as performed by Martha and extended to the poor are necessary out of our Love for Jesus. However in His presence we are right to attend upon Him, listen to Him and lavish our love upon His bodily presence. This is the lesson of Martha and Mary and the precious ointment poured out upon his head.*

Goodbye, dearest sister, for just a little while longer. Your Barque is nearing port. The breezes filling its sails are gentle airs of love. They are breezes that speed more swiftly than the lightning flash. Goodbye! In a few days we shall be together within the walls of Carmel, then afterwards in Paradise!

Did not Jesus say during His Passion, "Then you shall see the Son of Man sitting on the right hand of the power of God and coming in the clouds from heaven"?

We shall be there!

NB: This is a page note by the author.

CHAPTER 17

THE SHOWER OF ROSES

One by one she plucked the petals
From her roses red and white.
Plucked them with her dying fingers
Kissed and strew them round His Face.

Envisioned before her, the face of sorrow,
His face disfigured like the leper
She hears the derision of their jeering
At the fairest of the human race.

Day by day, Therese of Carmel
Like a flower on Calvary
Gave to the stricken Jesus
The sweet perfume of her tender love.

Gave to Him her love of innocence
and sweet bundles of unseen sacrifice.
Love in such abundance has no rivals
Even from those in Paradise.

From Tabor's heights she speaks of
the little doctrine of His way of love.
It is Christ who picks the roses
for the angel of His Face.

Swift the seraph casts them for her
Over Eden's jewelled walls.
From East to West, a storm of blossoms
Thick as snow these rose flakes fall.

From her fingers, fluttering, falling
This perfumed shower softly descends.
White petals for scarlet souls in sorrow
Red petals of love for her friends.

When her little souls are sad
she comes down, our precious queen.
Herself, she brings to earth her roses
restoring earth to Eden's scene.

Thus she keeps her burning promise:
'I, the little flower of Carmel,
shall spend my time in heaven,
doing good as the Rose Queen,
till earth's sorrows pass away.'

(T. N. Taylor)

"I will spend my heaven doing good upon earth. In heaven, God will do all I desire, because I have never done my own will on earth. After my death, I will cause a shower of roses to come down."

"Rome has spoken," and in the memorable phrase which heralded the Pontifical decision on 17th May 1925, Peter spoke through the voice of Pius XI that Therese of the Child Jesus was one of God's Saints.

Pius XI pronounced that rarely does God enrich His Church with someone who is both a 'miracle of virtues' and a 'prodigy of miracles'. The miracles, or 'Roses', to use her own charming and prophetic expression, are in the profoundest sense, the continuing chapters of her autobiography. They fill the air with the perfume that flows from her compassionate love, her delicate sympathy and her perpetual gaiety. Her love for Jesus and Mary and all her loved ones is passionately beautiful, like a riot of roses in June.

Her autobiography will only be complete when the last soul has entered the gates of heaven. For she desires to labour for God and He will refuse her nothing who refused Him nothing on earth. Therefore, the reign of our little Queen has no end. The following deposition to the Carmel of Lisieux, from an anonymous writer, shows that Saint Therese does not limit her Roses to those of the household of faith.

This letter is dated 14th July 1924
The Little Flower of Jesus has deigned to stoop down to me although I am a member of the Anglican Church and I must publish in her praise, that she has brought me back from the brink of hell.

I always had at heart, a sincere love of God, but the demon of impurity took possession of me from my early adulthood. What a martyrdom this grievous struggle was to me for more than sixteen years. I shudder yet when I think of the numerous defilements with which I sullied my soul. I tried to resist the evil, but so strong was the grip it had on me, that I always fell back again. Finally my Anglo-Catholic confessor, weary of so much wickedness, ended by refusing to direct me any longer and this abandonment of my soul plunged me into despair.

It was then that I made up my mind to read the life of the Blessed Therese of the Child Jesus. Bitter were the tears I shed when I came in contact with the 'Little White Flower'. What a contrast between the spotless purity of her soul and the vileness of mine! So powerful was the impression made upon me that I became ill through remorse. I threw myself upon my knees and begged my Saviour to have pity on me. "Only a miracle can save me," I cried, "for I have promised oh, so many times, to resist temptation but I have never succeeded. O my God, send to my aid your Little Therese." Then immediately, I felt beside me a mysterious presence and I heard the sweet voice of the Little Flower whisper in my ear, "See what divine grace has done for me. It will do as much for you if you are faithful to it." "O Saint of God," I replied, "I am at the end of my strength. If you would save me, you must fight with me and for me." And the voice from heaven replied, "I will do so. I will aid you with all my power."

For several days I had the happiness of feeling the sensible presence and continual assistance of the sweet Saint and I spent my time entirely in her company. My wretchedness had been changed into joy, when there occurred one of those occasions of sin which up until that time, I had been unable to resist. Just as I was on the point of giving way, I turned to her for help. "O Therese," I prayed, "save me in spite of myself." Then I conquered!

Instantly the devil took to flight. Nine months have passed since that day and Therese has kept her promise. Is it any wonder then that I love her beyond measure? If she delights to be the Little Flower of Jesus, may she permit me, in spite of my unworthiness, to be the 'little flower of Therese', that she may nurse me in her garden for the God of infinite mercy.

Irish Rose

This narrative comes from the pen of Professor Patrick Beecher, MA, DD, of Maynooth College in Ireland:

After a long search, I traced the family, Mrs Fitchett, her daughter and Miss Hennessy, sister to Mrs Fitchett. They are very poor and live in a single room next to the Holy Faith Convent in Strand Street. I got the following facts respectively from Mrs Fitchett, Miss Hennessy and Laura.

Mrs Fitchett:

"Laura was suffering from kidney trouble (acute nephritis) and dropsy and her body was swollen to twice its normal size. For six weeks she had taken no solid food. The Doctor (Dr Garland) said there was absolutely no hope. For three days she was unconscious and she was anointed for death, as there was no hope from medicine. I prayed to Blessed Therese and not only prayed but cried to her. Still the child became worse and had all the appearance of death. I was standing by the bed with my sister and two brothers. We could feel no pulse and we came to the conclusion that she was dead. One of my brothers put a mirror to her mouth and then said, 'She is not yet dead as there is moisture on the mirror.' I then felt a stifling feeling and had to leave the room as I could not bear to see Laura die and I also had no holy candles or other things for the wake. Still, at every step I took, I prayed to the little flower and said, 'It is not yet too late; won't you please send one of your Roses and cure my Laura?' I was out for about three-quarters of an hour and on my return, saw my sister standing at the door. I knew what that meant – Laura was dead! She said, 'I have news for you, Laura is cured.' When I came in Laura was sitting up in bed and said, 'Mother, I am cured. Get me my clothes, I want to get up and I'm starved with hunger!' I was afraid to let her get up and made her stay in bed to the following day but she appeared perfectly well and was craving every half-hour for food. I didn't want to give her as much as would satisfy her, as she had been so long without solid food."

Miss Hennessy:

"We were around the bed, just as my sister has described, waiting for Laura's death. My sister here, had gone out and there remained my two brothers and myself. Laura had all the appearance of death, but suddenly, a thrill passed through her and she sat up in bed, joined her hands and said three Hail Marys aloud and bowed her head profoundly at the Holy Name. She then stared at the other side of the bed away from us and we knew that she was gazing at some invisible person, because her eyes were bright and her whole face was beaming and she was drawn in that direction. One of my brothers spoke to her but I beckoned him to keep quiet. Next, she reached out her hand, apparently in the act of shaking hands and followed with her eyes halfway around the bed. Not only did she follow with her eyes but she was drawn in that direction and her face was beaming."

Coming now to Laura's own account of the incident, I should, first of all, say that she was a very mild little girl, with a frank open face, very shy and apparently incapable of inventing a story. She was then thirteen years of age and is now seventeen. She is not an intelligent child and the mother says, "She could never manage sums when at school." I impressed on Laura, as indeed on the mother and aunt too, the great wrong of saying anything that did not really happen. They understood that perfectly.

Laura said:

"Blessed Therese appeared beside the bed and the Blessed Virgin was beside her. She said, 'Sit up, Laura, and say three Hail Marys in honour of the Blessed Virgin.' Then she said, 'Bow to the Blessed Virgin,' and I bowed. She had a lovely white silk bag on her left arm and she opened it and took out a large white rose and put it to my nose to smell and then put it back again. Then she shook hands with me and said, 'Goodbye now, Laura, you are cured.' Then they both walked round the bed and when they came to that spot, I couldn't see them any longer."

I cross-examined the child most carefully; looking not only for the reply, but for the way it was given and it was that of one who has seen with her eyes.

"Did the Blessed Virgin say anything to you?"

"No, but she smiled when I bowed to her."

"What did she look like?"

"She had a blue mantle but she didn't have any crown."

"Of course, Laura, this was all a dream."

"Oh no, no, it was no dream – I saw her."

"Well, what happened was this – you were delirious and you fancied that she came out of that picture on the wall."

(The picture represented Saint Therese as a nun.)

"Oh no, I wasn't, and she was not like any picture I ever saw."

"What was she like?"

"A little girl in First Communion dress with a white wreath on her head and she had curls and a white silk bag on her left arm."

"Did you really feel her hand when she shook hands with you?"

"Yes, I did."

I may add that the mother tells me Laura is constantly speaking of the lovely white hands of the Little Flower. The fact remains that Laura was instantly cured and has never been ill since.

P. A. Beecher.

In this interview Laura describes her visit by the Blessed Virgin Mary and Saint Therese. The description she recalls so vividly of Saint Therese is of a child with a floral white wreath in a communion dress with curls and a white silk bag on her left arm.

This portrait is preserved on a photo plate which was not seen in public in the British Isles until at the earliest the 1920s. It is now a well known portrait of Saint Therese but could not have been seen in Ireland at the time of Laura's visitation by Our Lady and Therese! This adds to the authenticity of this miracle.

LITTLE THERESE

The Spirit of Love, the Love of the Father for the Son
The Spirit of Love, third person of the Adorable Trinity
Reigned ever in your heart, little flower of Jesus.
Plucked from the walled garden of your Father's heart
You travelled the Royal road and won the Palm.
The Palm remains, fresh forever, your precious gift.
Love is a treasure given, poured out never finished.
When the first petal of love of self heralds the real blossoming
Then the bud bursts and petals open with their perfume.
For this is selfless love, the first petal covered in the cup
It hides now with the diamond dewdrop.
The roses of her heart are scattered now across the Universe
The perfume of this damask Rose
Is the prayer of love, distilled perfection.
The precious gift of a heart overflowing
That never ceased to please her Lover.
Beloved, she was Beloved of Him, her Beloved.
In such unity her heart was melted,
Refined as dewdrops on her petalled lips,
Where He lived as the Word spoken,
The treasure trove of all her teaching.
That Love lived, were her dying words,
A greeting as she went above to meet Him.
But she comes back to teach her novices
The flower-strewn path of a pilgrim's longing.
Little Therese, calm us with your petal hands,
Hush our lips and let our hearts speak louder,
Teach us how to give our sins and sorrows

To Jesus so that He can hallow those hard bleak corners of our hearts.
When we give all, then we are all in Him.
There we'll meet you in love so beautiful
That we shall kiss you on your lips
And reach to kiss His Holy Face, so lovely,
That here with us, still droops from the Cross, in sorrow.
The chestnut trees are sticky with their buds
And we shall race to meet them, hand in hand with you.
Seeing them, a lovely sacrifice you offered,
We will recall the perfection of His hand.
Little Therese, rose of His heart,
That Sacred Heart, heart of His Church,
We offer your petals as our prayer
And our petals, our sacrifices here.
We long to greet you with a kiss in heaven
Where the choirs sing, we shall see Him as He is.

Amen.

BWF.

CHAPTER 18

MEDITATIONS FROM SAINT THERESE OF THE CHILD JESUS

T HE PERFECT; IT IS WHAT IT IS. There can be no 'more' perfect. This is a contradiction in terms. Anything and everything has the potential to be perfect, the capacity to be perfected. All can become perfect. Jesus Christ was and is the perfect being, the perfect human being was God, made in the image and likeness of God, He was perfect man and God. God is Spirit, therefore we know that mankind enspirited in the perfection of the unity of the Holy Spirit can come to God in that perfected state. The spirit of life envelops all living things and man, made in the image and likeness of God, is like God, not in His Power and Glory, but in His perfection for we can become perfect in Christ, through Christ and with Christ. The Incarnation has made our perfection not just possible but actual in His death and Resurrection.

Death of our temporal bodily state begins the process of the final stage of perfection. It is like the seed becoming detached from the living body, leaving that of which it was once part to fade away in decay and to return to the constituent dust from which it was created. The seed of our humanity, the spirit of life, grows to its perfection. The husk, the flesh, the detritus of life's decay falls away to form the nutrients of the seedbed. This is a way in which we can understand Purgatory. It is a stripping bare of the sweet decay of the corruption of the flesh, forming a nursery bed of nutrient for a perfect life – the new life, the new man, flooded with the moisture of the Spirit of Love, forcing the embryo seed, the potency of our perfection, to grow into a perfected body. The new man, perfect like Jesus Christ, flourishes eternally uncorrupted, at last the creature of God's creation, perfect in His image and likeness, humble before His Power and Glory. We shall see Him as He is, the perfect creature beholding the source of all perfection.

As creatures of spirit, living in the spiritual body of Christ, wrapped in the Holy Spirit, we can only be reborn in our true nature which is embodied Spirit, beyond and outside time. The shutters, the cage of time came down when 'we in Adam' turned away from God and sought the Power and Glory of God in His Justice, Wisdom, Light and unblemished and never-ending love, as our own possession rather than the everlasting gift of God. Time is the absolute dimension of mortality. It measures the effluxion processes of decay and ever-changing change. Time stakes out the limits of the Universe, not the limits of space but the fading processes of material flux. All creation is destined to be enspirited, stripped bare and reassembled in robes of light. Thus illuminated and infused, we shall be like the transparent winged bodies of the dragonfly but freed from time's shuttered eye. As time falls away before us, the past ceases to shade our view like the shadow at noon and all now is present and all present is now.

Thus we shall be freed from the shuttered cage of time. For the Universe is like a sleeve ravelled up which when removed falls in a heap without shape or form. Then we shall see the creative power of His arm and know the true force of His love. The ravelled sleeve of the Universe draws us to search and measure like blind mice, our learned faculties twitching like whiskers twitching in the dark. That big bang, the vast upheaval of the galaxies, was caused by the mere thought, executed by His Word. When we in Adam joined the galaxies, we fettered ourselves in the mortal framework of death. Light and space differentiate the dense darkness of nothingness, the silent implosion of non-existence, the black hole of death.

We walked once in Paradise, in the unfettered freedom of light, free to lead all His Creation to the eternity of His home. We failed, in Adam, to be saved in Christ, for all Creation is personified in Him. He has raised humanity to His heavenly state, freed in death from the shuttered cage of time; we shall walk in Paradise again, unless of course, we choose to remain in the cold bleak nothingness beyond the fires of a collapsing Universe running down the final eclipse of death and decay. For as the shadow passes and time is no more, there the divine light shines all in all.

CHAPTER 19

SUFFERING, PAIN AND LOSS

SUFFERING, PAIN AND LOSS ARE THE SIGNPOSTS of the decay and decrepitude of material existence disintegrating.

These signs of suffering, pain and loss overwhelm our senses, clog and dry up the emotional response of our hearts and render us victims, crying out for help. They are the continual reminders to reason and to the intellect that material existence is a pathway of death, destruction and renewal, of harvests, of food chains, of a struggle for life. Life, the gossamer thread so fine and unalterable that it cannot be located. Life, a pulsing rhythm in living things, centres our being in an array of senses through which we engage, interpret and sense the world around and thence come to know it.

Pain is signalled to us as a curtailment, a threat to the full functioning of our being in life. Just as brakes squeal when locked rather than proceeding in motion, so too the human physical and mental presence cries out as the living organ is threatened, curtailed or impaired. Suffering is caused by the many forms of malfunction, by misuse, abuse, decay, misalignment, collision, severance, excessive cold or heat, lack of nourishment, confinement or restriction. Just as the wheels are a functioning part of the driveline, they are integral to the vehicle; in their malfunctioning there is the possible linked event of the vehicle overturning and the passengers being fatally injured. Just so with suffering, pain and loss; it is the whole person who feels and suffers and in the integration of the emotional, the physical and the sensual material body, the deprivation and impairment known, felt and experienced, impinges on the living awareness of the sensory body. Life then, known within the physical limits of material experience, is threatened by cessation of its functioning.

If we are self-sufficient in the material reality of the human person, then we must acknowledge that this is due to natural, known scientific laws inherent in all material things and living structures. To the materialist then, this is accepted as an inevitable consequence of the material order of things and, therefore, the materialist acts rationally, the matter should be understood and accepted. Given adequate sources of energy and sufficient time, all matter will be recycled, and if procreation is purely a matter of life evolving with life infused within it, then there should be no perceived problem. As sentient animals, we are part of a very complex material process governed, ultimately, by the second law of thermodynamics. All things disintegrate and decay to be reassembled, composed into some other form of structure, some of which have the embodiment of life. For the materialist then, and the atheist, as I understand them, suffering, pain and loss are the consequence of evolutionary processes which could be explained as a design fault, a flawed process or just the necessary consequence of change which opens up the possibility of an evolutionary process through which living bodies become fitter to survive, better adapted to multiply as a species family, to a place and condition of dominance. From the scientific, materialist understanding then, there will evolve a dominant species which, as dominant and self-propagating, will remain dominant forever. Or should we say, until the end.

If this is indeed the position, it should be asked – what end? Why do we dread suffering, pain and loss and why be appalled by death? The survival of the species is not served by keeping the sick and old, the diseased and suffering, alive. The disabled are not served if they suffer in life and the species is not enhanced by their possible genetic flaws. Logic, that is restricted scientific logic, the logic of understanding all things as material objects, explains the senses and emotions as phenomena reactive of material functioning and no more. This logic, as a purported rational understanding of human existence, calls into question   all forms of healthcare and strongly supports all those who argue that only the strong and healthy should live and propagate the species. All other human beings should be allowed to perish or be put to death. The practice of medicine then, would be based on the understanding that only the strong and fit should be nursed and cared for and then only if they were judged to be able, consequently, to serve the overriding purpose of the dominant survival of the species. This was, and is in part, the political philosophy of all the utilitarian and Utopian political movements. The names of these 'political' leaders is most evocative – Mao Tse Tung, Stalin, Hitler, Pol Pot, Lenin and a hundred others. Behind them stand the philosophers, Marx, Engels, Feurerbacher, Hobbs, Nietzsche and the rest. These scientific thinkers formulated a set of theories of the understanding of humankind within an historic process of pain, loss and suffering by the masses that served the wilful dominance of a self-propagating elite. These scientific theories were then proposed to the masses and put into practice with much popular acclaim. The theories were tested from the early nineteenth century until presently, to the end of the twentieth century. With what result? – total human misery and disaster and, rationally, the demise of the utilitarian and Utopian philosophies based on a materialistic scientific understanding of human life should be a reality. On the contrary, these theories enshrined in law and put into practice by Nazi and communist regimes alike survive and are propagated by enthusiasts demanding the right to commit euthanasia, widespread abortion on demand, mercy killing of the old, the infirm, the mentally disabled and the right to put to death those of the 'wrong' sex.

The tyrants of the past, of empire and national aggrandisement seeking dominion, wealth and greater power, came through, survived and were defeated by force of arms. Armies and navies contested for supremacy and wars resulted in political settlements. Power was shared out, people subjected and political rivalry continues.

The ideologies that were used were often religious ideas supporting legitimate authority and were thus constrained to understand humanity as unique individuals, created and sustained in life by a living God. Thus pain, loss and suffering could only be the result of the self-harming consequence of sin which followed from the rebellion against a loving, compassionate God by humankind seeking self-understanding and an all-knowing grasp of creation which would enable humankind to dominate all creation in perpetuity. Is this the destiny of the human race? If so, what are we to do about pain, loss and suffering? To the scientific materialist they are mere

242

matters of accident, the chance aberration of 'magnificent complex material processes'. To the evolutionary theorist, they are part of a natural process, which should enable us to ensure the survival of the fittest, to ensure the perpetual dominance of the human species. We should heed the lessons of history but follow broadly the methods pioneered by those notable humanitarians, Adolf Hitler and Joseph Stalin!

However, what of suffering, pain and loss within a Christian context, namely God's Plan of Salvation? How can we understand such pointless and negative experiences in the all-embracing love of God?

Suffering, pain and loss are in this era identified as negative experiences, which serve no purpose and invariably cause unhappiness. They are understood and realised as contrary to the normal, healthy human condition. However, more difficult to address are pain, loss and suffering experienced out of proportion to the individual's age, circumstance and reasonable expectation. As I have remarked beforehand, these expectations are an irrational response to the human condition within the rational understanding of the atheistic, rational, scientific humanism. The question can only be proposed as difficult phenomena of human life, as understood in a religious and specifically Christian way of life.

Before considering the questions related to suffering, pain and loss from a Christian way of living, we must first distinguish the Christian knowledge of the human person from all other ways of knowing humankind.

Predominant in Christian Teaching is the understanding that humanity is distinguished, not as a dominant species, but rather as embodied spiritual persons created by the Creator of all things, which is God, God the Father, the giver of life. As embodied spiritual persons, we are members of a community inhabiting the Universe which He created out of nothing, that is unordered matter devoid of life – cold, silent and dead. From the dust of His creation, out of nothing, He brought forth life and fashioned humankind in His image, of love and likeness, of life. It is known then, as revealed to Christians, that humankind is a community of embodied spiritual persons born in the love of God into an embodied life in the created Universe, a spiritual creation of personhood endowed with the life and love of the Creator. Time and the history of human events are the way in which the material Universe will come to know salvation with God. His saving grace provides a pathway for the Universe to remain in existence with Him yet not part of Him. As all-powerful, He seeks the total abnegation of that power over creation so that universal creation, out of loving freedom, can come to Him in a perfect unity of being which is everlasting life with Him. In creation, humankind was made for Paradise with Him. That is the beginning and the end; yet there must be a process for the material created Universe with humankind to be perfected and evolve in that process to the perfection of Paradise. Paradise where the spiritual embodiment of life will exist in harmony; that is, to walk and talk with God, where God, who is Spirit, can be with His creatures in a harmony of existence. This forming, out of chaotic material nothingness, of an embodied spiritual human race, is the wonder of a new creation out of the material and the spiritual. The clearest manifestation of human spirituality is mankind's emotional, intellectual use, in understanding, of the creative purpose of music and language. As the body becomes subordinate to our spiritual existence and our spiritual existence takes hold of our bodies, in its perfection, so death becomes the resurrection to life in the fullness of His Creation.

Thus we come to understand our mortal death in the same way as suffering, pain and loss. In terms of a limited material existence, death limits our experience of suffering, pain and loss. This allows us, within this limited horizon, to view all death, suffering, loss and pain as passing events within a very lengthy process.

However, in the Christian way of knowing, these anguishing phenomena must be understood within the understanding of the Salvific Plan of God.

In this view, creation is a saving process whereby the material Universe will be transformed in a spiritual creation and exist with God; not as part of Him and His existence, but rather existent from Him, to be with Him out of freedom in love.

Humankind, as Adam and Eve, created out of material dust, comes to Paradise as spiritually embodied persons and comes to view the knowledge of created things as giving them parity with the Creator. However, this knowledge is limited to life as known through and of material things. They are creatures; that is, themselves, a material creation, and in this is their alienation from the spiritual existence of God and an overweening attachment to material things, their nature and the understanding of the laws which govern them, the so-called scientific laws which are much better understood as natural laws. Thus humankind, caged and fettered within the limited framework of knowing, seeks, in the absence of his full human spiritual relationship with God, dominion over the material Universe, over and against our loving creation, not out of the freedom of love in order to serve our loving God in His creation made good, but rather, out of the arrogance in the assumption of humankind's right to dominate the material Universe. This trajectory leads, logically, to mankind assuming the functioning role of creator and judge of the material Universe. This materialistic, atheistic, humanistic understanding of the destiny of humankind, in the Christian way of understanding, has set mankind against God. Mankind assumes the role of creator and judge in direct opposition to our Loving God who ministers only saving justice. This opposition to God's love in creation causes harm throughout the human race. It has been called original sin but is as apparent and widespread as can be imagined in our own times. This opposition and rebellion manifests itself in all kinds of ways from generation to generation. The vast proportion of suffering, pain and loss is caused by aberrant human behaviour, manifest in pollution, in wars and conflict, disease and maltreatment of the poor and vulnerable. This human condition is like the opium addict dreaming the dream of the conquest of harmony whilst dying of neglect and malnutrition. Only to the Christian is there a struggle to understand suffering, pain and loss as opposed to their way of knowing God as a Loving God acting always in Saving Justice.

When we know suffering, pain and loss, the Christian knows himself as impaired and restricted in the flesh. The flesh, however, in this life, dominates and often prostrates the emotions, renders the intellect dull and inactive and the understanding of our spiritual being and existence recedes and is known in impoverishment. We are not ourselves, whole and entire, but rather alien from ourselves, broken and diminished. However, when we meditate upon this human understanding of loss, we must first note that in the fullness of being, we retain a self-vision without which we could not know of suffering, pain and loss. This self-visualisation and knowledge cannot be merely physical, for we are recalling that which is no longer existent in form or feeling. Recalling our childhood does not enable us to become a child once more. Our self-vision transcends this material, physical existence and draws us to the threshold of a spiritual, sensory awareness. The hard reality of this sensual, material existence begins to melt and sway, to recede from and encroach into our living space. Our perception of this existent reality falters and the self-vision of our spiritual existence comes into view.

However degrading and gratuitously suffering pain and loss come to us, they confirm us in our humanity. The limbless, the paralysed, the mentally afflicted, the cripple, the epileptic and those with other afflictions are, without question, unique in their humanity. As a community and individuals, our loss and their suffering do not shut up the reservoir of the love of God or our love for one another. Pain, loss and suffering are signal reminders of our understanding of being whole and entire and the possibility of perfection.

In this process of becoming perfect in Paradise with God is a process of conflict, embodied in humankind's spiritual tranquillity, which is set to engulf and transform the turbulent, transient order of the physical Universe, but like childbirth, out of suffering, pain and loss, comes new life. As a physical process, all life processes through decay and loss to suffering because of the unstable nature of the physical matter being transformed, in humankind, to the spiritual reality of life existent in love becoming complete as a spiritual actuality present before God. Thus, through the Spirit, we become spiritual beings in our resurrected bodies in Christ because, as God made flesh, the flesh is divinised in God who is Spirit.

God, incarnate through suffering, pain and loss, transforms our unstable, volatile humanity into the perfection of spiritual beings like God.

This Christian way of knowing is illumined by the fullness of God's revelation throughout history, completed and fulfilled in the life and works of Jesus the Nazarene, the Messiah, the Word made Flesh, as proclaimed in the New Testament and Tradition of the Holy Spirit sent to His Apostles and disciples, His mystical body, His Universal Church.

The Church of Saint Therese. The Little White Flower; where she with all the Heavenly Host tends upon this vale of tears preparing the towel with which He will wipe away our tears.

To this we attest Truly, Truly

Amen, Amen.

Reading List

The Little White Flower Cannon T.N.Taylor [this is the main source of texts which are contained in this book]

Catechism of the Catholic Church [May 1994, Geoffrey Chapman]

Roman Missal page V

Insight by Bernard J. F. Lonnergan

Commentary on the Gospels Aquinas, Saint Luke.

The Jerusalem Bible

The Autobiography of Therese de Lisieux Edited by Robert Backhouse